THE NEW MONEY RULES

The New Money Rules

THE GEN Z GUIDE TO PERSONAL FINANCE

Lillian Zhang

callisto
publishing
an imprint of Sourcebooks

Published by Callisto Publishing LLC C/O Sourcebooks LLC
P.O. Box 4410, Naperville, Illinois 60567-4410
(630) 961-3900
callistopublishing.com

Library of Congress Cataloging-in-Publication Data is on file with the publisher.

Printed and bound in the United States of America.
VP 10 9 8 7 6 5 4 3 2 1

CONTENTS

INTRODUCTION

I learned about the value of money after starting my first small business at ten years old: selling plushies. I turned my hobby of making cute stuffed animals at home into some pocket money by taking them to school and selling them to my classmates. To my amazement, it worked!

Soon, I was knocking on doors in my apartment complex to sell my products to neighbors and making YouTube videos to market my creations. I even participated every year at my middle school's annual craft fair. In my first year at the fair, I made a whopping $500, which was *a lot* to my young brain.

What did I do with my plushie fortune? I put part of it in savings and treated myself to some UGG boots and high-end Copic Markers (I know, 11-year-old me had bougie taste). Even as a kid, I was learning to make choices about earning, saving, and spending. This experience laid the foundation for my ongoing interest in personal finance.

My parents were the first to show me the value of hard work. They emigrated from China to the United States in the 1980s, hoping for a better life and a more prosperous future than what was possible in their homeland. Even though we didn't have much growing up, their biggest gift to me was my education. In the mid-2000s, we moved from the Midwest to California, renting a one-bedroom apartment. My parents decided to rent for ten years in the best school district instead of buying a home. This allowed them to save money so that I could go to college. I'm so grateful that my parents instilled in me the value of hard work and nurtured every interest I had. I firmly believe in education and its ability to change your family story—including reading finance books like this one!

Don't get me wrong, money was often a stressful topic in our household. I heard my fair share of my parents' arguments over money growing up. More than anything, my parents wanted me

to have access to opportunities and security that hadn't come so easily for them. Despite our circumstances, they worked hard to help me open these doors.

Isn't that how things are meant to go? Each new generation enjoys a better life than their parents did, right? Unfortunately, today, that belief system is increasingly untrue. With the rising cost of living, explosive student loan debt, and high housing prices, indicators show that Gen Z—those born between 1997 and 2012—could be the first generation in modern history to be *worse* off than their parents.

I know that I've been one of the lucky ones. Despite—or possibly because of—the stress of money growing up, I became highly motivated to learn how to manage and grow my earnings as an adult. I expanded my business and finance knowledge while at the Haas School of Business at the University of California, Berkeley, where I earned my Bachelor of Science degree. I've also worked at leading tech companies and started a successful business. In my early twenties, I saved my first $100,000. I started posting on social media to share what I had learned and experienced. Now, I offer career and money education to hundreds of thousands on TikTok, Instagram, and YouTube.

Interacting with my community, I've noticed that the biggest issue facing young people is a lack of financial literacy. It's bizarre that we spend so much of our life in school preparing ourselves for the real world, such as getting a job, earning a paycheck, and finally being independent. Yet, no one teaches us how to manage our finances wisely. This lack of education means that money can feel scary and complicated as an adult, so I decided to write this book.

THE NEW RULES OF PERSONAL FINANCE

As a member of Gen Z myself, I was surprised that there aren't any books out there specifically for our generation. After all, we are experiencing many unique economic factors that are different from previous generations. The housing market looks different, and the job market, too—not to mention other stuff to wrap your head around, like robo-advisors, micro-investing platforms, cryptocurrency, meme stocks, digital "buy now, pay later" services, the temptation of online shopping on social media—just to name a few!

With this book, I hope to share the ins and outs of financial literacy in a way that makes sense for young people today. You won't find finger-wagging advice about skipping your vanilla lattes (or avocado toast) to build wealth. Instead, you'll encounter helpful insights about how to feel more confident with your money—no matter where you're starting from. My goal is to help you make smart money moves now so that you can start planning for a better financial future.

Each chapter of the book covers a different area of personal finance, including navigating earnings, budgeting, savings, debts, loans, and investing. I tackle all the basics, updating them for the realities of today. I offer new rules for gaining control of your personal finances—whether it's the psychology of money, using online tools to level up your budget, thinking strategically about home ownership, or starting to invest your money using digital platforms.

Please think of me as your financially responsible bestie, sharing realistic and empowering guidance for our generation to earn, budget, save, and invest, even in the face of a system that isn't always tipped in our favor.

I must acknowledge that I'm not a financial advisor, and this book is for educational purposes only. However, I strongly believe that knowledge is power. I want to equip you with all the information you need to feel energized about putting your financial future into your own hands so you can live a more comfortable life—now and beyond.

①

THE GEN Z FINANCIAL RESET

I f you're reading this book, chances are you are in your twenties or about to enter them. This is the decade in your life where you go from being a student of life to a participant. Everyone is on the same path: going to school, doing homework, taking exams, and hanging out after class. Then, suddenly, you're thrust into the real world, where the possibilities are endless, and the path forward isn't so clear. It's exciting but also overwhelming. Some days, I feel like I've got adulting down, while other days, I still feel like I'm a kid pretending to be a grown-up.

While entering adulthood has never been easy, it can feel extra confusing for Gen Z, especially regarding personal finance. The rules of the game have changed, from the economy to technology, and it's not always clear how best to get by with our money, let alone get ahead.

So what's the good news? Only when you understand how the rules have changed compared to your parents or grandparents—and how to think differently about your money—can you adapt your thinking and decision-making to start growing your wealth.

In this chapter, we'll look at the big picture for Gen Z and explain why this group needs to think differently about money than previous generations. In the following chapters, I'll walk you through how to approach the key areas of personal finance—including earnings, savings, taking on debt, and investing, among others—so you can map out a game plan for a brighter financial future. You'll learn what age-old financial advice stands the test of time and what new rules to follow.

You have the power to chart your course. So, let's get started!

THE BIG PICTURE FOR GEN Z

As Gen Zers we are navigating a world filled with unique challenges, from the aftermath of a global pandemic to the rapid rise in technological advancements. Here's a quick list of what our generation is dealing with:

Rising student loans: Student debt is a massive weight on our shoulders. With skyrocketing college tuition and costs, many of us are graduating with more debt than previous generations. In the United States, the average student loan debt is over $38,000, making buying a home or even living comfortably feel out of reach. Paying off these loans often becomes the main focus, delaying other big life moves, like starting a family or returning to school.

Housing affordability: Let's be real: Wages haven't kept up with the cost of housing for more than four decades. For many in our generation, the dream of owning a home feels increasingly out of reach. Renting is the new norm, but even that comes with sky-high prices that leave little room for savings. It can be tricky to make ends meet while saving for the future.

Economic uncertainty: We all saw how the economy took a hit after the COVID-19 pandemic. Recent grads are finding it difficult to break into the job market. Inflation has pushed up prices, and paychecks don't stretch as far as they used to.

Technology's double-edged sword: We grew up with smartphones and social media, which can be both a blessing and a curse. Sure, they've opened doors to side hustles and the gig economy, but they've also become a never-ending comparison game. It's easy to get caught up in what everyone else is doing with their lives, their futures, and their money. It can mess with your mental health.

Ongoing inequality: Some of us face these challenges differently. People of color, women, and LGBTQIA+ folks in our generation often deal with systemic barriers like wage gaps, discrimination in the job market, and limited access to affordable housing or quality education.

Patchy financial literacy: The lack of financial education in schools can make these problems feel even more overwhelming. Knowing where to start when learning to budget, invest, or manage essential finances is complicated.

I'm glad you've decided to take the initiative to start to understand how to navigate these obstacles. Learning to manage your money smartly is the best gift you can give yourself. You will always have these tools, enabling you to make informed financial decisions that secure your future.

Gen Z Reality Check

As I was writing this book, I reached out to my online community to measure how they view handling finances in today's world through a Gen Z lens. I've collected several interesting comments. You'll notice they're sprinkled throughout the book, showing the realities of what our generation is facing. As you read through the book, you may see a theme. Managing money for our generation looks very different than it did for previous generations. I am convinced that a fresh approach to financial literacy is needed more than ever.

> "I feel that I wasn't taught how to use money for pretty much all of high school... I feel very unprepared to start working and go into college/be an adult."
>
> —Mohr, 18 years old

> "As a member of Gen Z with parents from the younger side of Gen X, I've noticed that a lot of the financial advice they offer doesn't quite fit today's realities. The financial literacy and strategies they relied on worked well in their time because their money stretched further."
>
> —Drew, 23 years old

> "The most challenging thing is not knowing where to start. It's like you want to get somewhere, and you know you need to work on learning, but there's too much information, and you get overwhelmed. They should have taught me this in school."
>
> —Jenny, 23 years old

OLD-SCHOOL MONEY ADVICE

Let's face it, the "old-school" rules of personal finance don't cut it anymore. For earlier generations, the advice for managing money was more straightforward but also rooted in different circumstances. It's hard to believe that just a few decades ago, a family could afford a house and a car and to raise kids on one income. Insane, right?! Ah, the simple times.

The financial advice for earlier generations emphasizes a "pull yourself up by your bootstraps" mentality. This approach also assumed that everyone had said boots. But this mindset doesn't recognize how much has changed. Here's some common "advice" many of us are tired of hearing:

"Don't keep switching jobs; stay loyal to one employer for as long as possible." Sometimes, I see older people look down on younger people's decision to change jobs after a couple of years. Earlier generations, especially baby boomers, benefited from greater job security in a time when loyalty was valued. It's common to hear of someone from that generation who worked at the same company for 30 years. Must be nice. But today? The job market is an entirely different beast. Job hopping is often a strategy to get a significant pay bump. Sticking around too long at one company could potentially stall your career growth.

"Home ownership should be your immediate goal." It used to be possible for people in their twenties to take their first step onto the housing ladder. Paying a mortgage was doable. But today, with skyrocketing housing prices and the rising cost of living, saving up for a down payment on a home has become increasingly difficult. Comparing your situation to that of previous generations can create unhealthy expectations about achieving this goal. Setting up unrealistic timelines can only lead to frustration and a sense that you're "falling behind." But there's no need to feel bad about living at home with your parents or renting. Doing so offers you a lot more flexibility. You don't have to worry about the maintenance of home ownership while planning for your financial future.

"Just live below your means, and everything will be fine." This is *mostly* still good advice, but it can feel out of touch for many people struggling with stagnant wages and high living costs. We can't ignore the cost of living has made it harder to stretch a paycheck. So yes, living below your means is important, but we also need to acknowledge that the "means" are much tighter than they used to be. Like it or not, we need to be more strategic about how we earn, save, and invest for the future.

"It's not a good look to talk about money openly." For a long time, people believed openly talking about money was taboo or rude. Gen Z is way more transparent and willing to share their experiences, especially on social media. This is also known as "loud budgeting" (when you openly share what fits in your budget and what doesn't), where people openly talk about how much is in their savings accounts. (For more on loud budgeting, see page 84.) Talking to a coworker about your salary was unheard of. You didn't do it. Some states have mandated employers to list a base salary range on job postings to promote pay transparency. It's more common for Gen Z to share how much they're getting paid with their coworkers, which can help lower the wage gap. Gen Z is much more open to discussing their pay because they have greater online access to information, making it more normal to share financial details (and help each other win).

"Don't make decisions about money without a financial advisor." Back in the day, learning about how to handle your money meant you had to turn to resources. The finance section of a newspaper or the help of a professional financial advisor was the only way. Now, with broad online access to information and the ability to do banking and invest money from a smartphone, financial decision-making is democratized.

The Truth About Your Iced Vanilla Lattes

I'm sure you've heard that Gen Z can't get ahead financially because they lack the willpower to resist indulgences like coffee at cafes. Let's test this theory, shall we?

Suppose you bought coffee five times a week for $5 a day. That would amount to $1,300 in a year. Yes, having that money back in your pocket is better than nothing. But do you think skipping out on morning coffee (or your tea or juice or...avocado toast) is the key to buying a house?

A lot of personal finance advice out there emphasizes saving every dollar you can, even if that deprives you of the small joys in life. Though it's usually well-meaning advice, it isn't realistic and sustainable in the long run. Truthfully, it feels out of touch. Many of you are working your butts off to make it in this economy. Shaming you into giving up the thing that gives you the TINIEST bit of happiness is not the solution.

Let's be clear: I'm not saying you *should* buy coffee every single day. However, whatever treat gives you joy is valuable because it is an investment in your overall happiness. If buying an iced vanilla latte from your favorite café every morning brings you joy, why give it up?

The big financial decisions—big-ticket spending decisions like housing and transportation, paying down debt, and finding ways to make more money—are what move your financial needle, not doing away with your daily latte. More on that in the following chapters!

A NEW ERA FOR GEN Z

The advice that worked for previous generations doesn't work as well as it used to. For Gen Z, it's not just about saving for a rainy day or clipping coupons like it was for past generations. (Though don't get me wrong; I do love a good deal.)

Our generation's approach to financial independence is more than acquiring stuff. The new money era for Gen Z is about making money decisions based on empowerment and security, not guilt and fear. We want to make financial goals that align with our values and lifestyle.

We grew up using technology our entire lives, and it's no different when it comes to using technology to manage our finances. With apps for budgeting, investing, and tracking expenses, managing finances has never been more accessible. The internet has also opened up many possibilities in the gig economy and online side hustles. This allows anyone—especially Gen Z—to build wealth in the modern digital economy and gain access to new opportunities that may not have been possible without our tech-driven world.

A lot of financial advice is based on fear and guilt. We need to *decenter* this mindset and shift our thinking toward using money to achieve security and freedom.

Many people say, "Money doesn't bring happiness," but I disagree. Money offers security, peace of mind, and the freedom to pursue your passions and escape toxic situations. But accumulating cash isn't the end-all-be-all; it's ultimately just a tool for building security and living life to the fullest.

This includes saving for emergencies, so you aren't constantly worried about paying next month's bills. When it comes to using credit, use it to your advantage. (Remember, not all debt is bad, but more on that later.) It can be used for big moves that will pay off down the line, like your education or your first house. Just be sure to steer clear of the high-interest debt that doesn't give you anything back.

Samantha Takes Control

At 23, Samantha found herself grappling with the newfound challenges of adulthood. Along with navigating a new city and getting settled at her new job, she was also trying to prioritize learning about personal finance. She didn't know about investing and budgeting money while in school. She started her search by stopping at her nearest bookstore's "Finance & Business" section. But after browsing through a few titles, she found it hard to relate to the advice from the authors. Most grew up during economic times that were much different from the realities of today. Not surprisingly, she left the store with many questions unanswered.

Determined to change her situation, she started by seeking out financial content specifically tailored to her generation. She followed influencers who broke down personal finance in bite-sized, practical tips. She then supplemented that learning with personal finance books that she could relate to. But despite all the new information she was absorbing, Samantha struggled to put it into practice and felt overwhelmed by the sheer volume of advice.

It wasn't until Samantha reframed her thinking that she began to make progress. Instead of expecting overnight mastery, she focused on small, realistic steps. First, Samantha automated small savings each month and explored beginner-friendly investment platforms. It helped her realize that financial empowerment wasn't about quick fixes or keeping up with others. It was about building a system that worked for her life, needs, and mindset. Samantha began to feel more in control, and her desire to build a solid foundation in financial literacy that will serve her for years.

THE ROAD MAP FOR YOUR TWENTIES

It's never too late to plan your financial vision, whether you're just starting or are more established. Planning and breaking down bigger concepts into smaller steps also helps make your finances more approachable.

I've mapped out a list of financial priorities for you to think about to set you up for a strong financial foundation for your twenties and beyond:

#1: Get Financially Literate

Educating yourself and developing your financial literacy is your financial road map's most important first step. It's like building the base of a house—if you don't have a solid framing, the house will fall apart. I'd recommend learning information from various sources: books (including this book, of course), online articles, podcasts, and YouTube videos. I suggest learning about tactical details first. These include intentional spending, how to manage your monthly income, investing 101, and more—all topics we will cover in this book. Improving your financial knowledge helps you build financial confidence. It's helpful to learn about something from different perspectives, and it enables you to develop your outlook, too. When people ask me how I learned about personal finance so early on, it was because I spent a good chunk of my free time looking up information (not me watching Graham Stephan videos at 1 a.m.!) while going through trial and error in terms of what worked for me.

#2: Invest in Yourself

Though it is essential to invest your money early, I believe it's arguably more important to invest in yourself, especially your skills and career. After all, you need to make money to save and invest it. Investing early in yourself will pay dividends in the future. Think about it this way: Your skills are your most valuable assets. Consider upskilling through education, whether it's through school, courses, or internships. Taking advantage of on-the-job training boosts your income potential and secures greater job security.

#3: Understand Your Debt

If you're in a situation where you're paying off debt, it's important to be strategic about paying it down while still balancing your present and future needs. Start by understanding the entire picture of your debt. Knowing what you owe is the first step toward managing it effectively. It can also be scary, but this step is vital. There are different strategies for paying down debt, like the snowball and the avalanche methods (we'll explore debt more in Chapter 5), plus strategies to refinance interest rates on your loans.

#4: Plan for Major Life Events

Your twenties are a time of adventure and exciting "firsts"—from exploring the world to buying your first car to finding true love and possibly planning a wedding. There are so many possibilities for you! These milestones are pretty exciting but can also get super pricey very quickly. Automated savings is a saving grace here. It's a no-brainer way to stash cash without thinking about it. Set up your checking account to sneak a part of your paycheck into a savings fund for a car down payment or house down payment. (You can learn more about automating savings on page 71.) And don't forget about building that emergency fund! Aim to put away about three to six months' living expenses. It's your financial safety net to catch you if a curveball like a job loss or unexpected medical bill comes your way. (More on this on page 61.)

#5: Cultivate a Healthy Money Mindset

Even though much of the talk about personal finance is about tactical tips and advice, it's also important to pay attention to the emotional side while cultivating a healthy money mindset. For instance, I often hear a lot of talk within the personal finance community about the things people shouldn't buy or should cut out from their lives. But it all comes down to spending on the areas of your life you care about and saving on things you don't care for as much. Also, don't forget the balance between saving for the future and enjoying your life now. If you're still prioritizing your financial goals, don't be too hard on yourself, and enjoy the present, too.

PUT IT INTO ACTION:
CREATING YOUR ROAD MAP

In this section, you will draft a road map based on your current financial situation. We will revisit this road map in Chapter 8 to see how your plan has evolved.

Step 1: Reflection Questions

Before you create your road map, take some time to reflect on your financial journey. Journal your responses to these questions:

What is your current financial situation? (Income, expenses, savings, debts)

_____

_____

_____

What are your short-term and long-term financial goals? Examples: saving for an emergency fund, paying off student loans, investing for retirement, buying a home, etc.

_____

_____

_____

What financial habits are you most proud of?

_____

_____

_____

Which ones would you like to change or improve?

_____

_____

_____

What's holding you back from achieving your financial goals right now?

_____

_____

_____

How do you currently feel about your relationship with money? Is it a source of stress or of empowerment?

_____

_____

_____

Step 2: Draft Your Road Map

Now that you've reflected, let's draft a road map that aligns with your financial goals. It doesn't need to be perfect. Focus on the following areas:

Short-term goals (1–2 years): What will you focus on first?

_____

_____

_____

_____

_____

Mid-term goals (3–5 years): Where financially do you want to be?

_____

_____

_____

_____

_____

_____

_____

Long-term goals (10+ years): What does financial freedom look like to you?

_____

_____

_____

_____

_____

_____

_____

_____

_____

_____

Remember, this road map is a draft. In Chapter 8 (page 183), you will revisit it to refine your plan as you proceed.

I also recommend keeping a money diary or journal to help you take notes from learnings throughout the book and how your mindset shifts over time!

FACT-CHECKING GEN Z MYTHS

Gen Z approaches life differently than previous generations but that's not bad! Let's clear up some of the common myths about us.

Myth: Gen Z Is Bad at Saving Money

Reality: Gen Zers are saving and investing on average at age 19, which is much younger than boomers who began at age 35. Millennials didn't start until age 25! This doesn't surprise me. Think how easy it is to get online financial info and tools compared to earlier generations.

Myth: Gen Z Isn't Loyal to Employers

Reality: While research shows that Gen Z workers are more likely to change jobs, it's not because they are disloyal. They want a clear path to career advancement and value work-life balance. But they are also savvy enough to know that moving to a new company can help them improve their job title and earn more.

Myth: Gen Z Doesn't Care About Education

Reality: Some people (looking at you, boomers) would have you believe that Gen Z spends all their time scrolling their smartphones rather than engaging in formal learning. But research shows that they are more likely than previous generations to finish high school and enroll in college.

Myth: Gen Z Is Entitled and Lazy

Reality: Boomers love to label younger folk as "participation trophy" generations for supposedly receiving awards in activities no matter if we win or lose. The idea is that we expect things to be handed to us without putting in effort. In reality, we are just as ambitious as those who came before us and far from blasé about our careers. We grew up during a global financial crisis and lived through a global pandemic; we are far from carefree about our place in the workforce. We know that doing the bare minimum won't provide us with job security.

LET'S TALK ABOUT PRIVILEGE

We can't talk about money without acknowledging privilege and its role in how it shapes our lives. Not everyone starts at the same starting line. Some people's parents help with things like college and housing, while others didn't have any financial support from their parents and had to take out student loans or work multiple jobs to make ends meet.

Maybe we all didn't grow up with the stereotypical idea of privilege, but for many of us, our surroundings or circumstances can shape how we view the world. For instance, the fact that you're reading this book right now means you have access to books and education. I was born in the United States, my parents had college degrees, and I grew up in a town with good public schools; these are all things I would consider my privileges.

People who've gone through difficult situations can have a greater appreciation of financial stability, or it may motivate them to work hard to achieve their goals. Maybe you grew up in a household where no one talked about money—except to stress about it. Or perhaps you've always had to be hyper-aware of every dollar you spend because you didn't have a financial safety net to fall back on. A lot can be learned from enduring financial hardship—you become more assertive about your financial choices as a result.

Some benefit from inheriting money or receiving financial support from family, but that's not the reality for many. Frankly, most people have to rely on themselves to build up their careers and finances; there's no safety net to fall back on. This doesn't mean you can't build your future and wealth—you can. It takes dedication, time, education, and patience. The resources are out there to help you. And the fact that you're reading this book, educating yourself, and taking control of your financial future is already a huge step in the right direction.

The playing field isn't level. But that doesn't mean you can't win your own game. Understanding where you're starting from can help you set realistic goals and create a plan to achieve them, no matter where you begin.

KNOWLEDGE IS POWER

Not everyone starts with a trust fund, but everyone can equip themselves with the knowledge to live a financially aware and fulfilling life. Like learning to write, financial literacy is a skill honed through repetition and practice.

Financial literacy helps you...

- **Build confidence.** Understanding how money systems work can transform your approach to money management. It's about controlling your money rather than letting it control you. This knowledge fosters confidence in your financial decisions, from daily spending to strategic investing.

- **Plan for your future.** Are you saving for big milestones—a car, vacation, wedding? Understanding how to manage your money for your present and medium- and long-term goals will help you set up a system to help you enjoy your life now while planning for the future.

- **Weather crises.** You could get laid off, need an unexpected medical procedure, or have unforeseen expenses—you never know what life could throw at you. Staying prepared for the unexpected alleviates some of the pressure you might be feeling and could empower you to do things and take risks that would be harder without a safety net.

Empowering yourself with financial knowledge benefits you and has ripple effects: It can help your parents retire comfortably, break generational cycles of financial strain, and foster economic stability in your community.

You've Got This!

When stepping up your financial game, mental blocks are arguably one of the biggest challenges. Do any of these sound like you?

- **"Personal finance sounds boring with all those complicated terms."** Don't worry; we're stripping away the jargon and making everything digestible. This isn't your typical finance textbook.

- **"I'm just not a numbers person. Don't you need to be good at math to be good with money?"** Good news: Managing your finances is more about consistent habits than complex math. You won't need anything beyond basic arithmetic—promise!

- **"Checking my bank account feels like bracing for bad news—I just can't."** We'll transform that dread into confidence by demystifying those numbers and showing you exactly what they mean and how you can manage them better.

This book will lay the groundwork in everyday terms, whether you're starting from scratch or looking to refine your skills.

As you explore each chapter of this book, take a moment to write down your financial fears or any misconceptions you've held about money. Reflect on how the chapters address these concerns, and challenge yourself to apply at least one new insight from each section to your daily life. By the end of this book, you will have a clearer understanding of personal finance and see how far you've come in overcoming those barriers that once seemed daunting. Let's start this journey together—your future self will thank you.

TAKEAWAYS
THE NEW RULES OF
PERSONAL FINANCE FOR GEN Z

With the rising cost of housing, education, and everyday living, the old-school rules of personal finance just don't cut it anymore. It's up to you to embrace financial literacy and think more strategically about how to earn, save, and invest for your future.

OLD RULES	NEW RULES
We can rely on our families and schools to learn financial literacy	Financial literacy isn't a given at home or school, but it's easier than ever to learn on your own
Gen Z expects a participation trophy just for showing up	Gen Z is just as ambitious and hardworking as previous generations
Simply live below your means to build wealth	Young people have to be more strategic than previous generations about earning, saving, and investing for the future
Treating yourself to small items like lattes will keep you broke	Gen Z isn't struggling because they enjoy lattes; it's because of big-picture economic challenges
You need professional help to improve your finances	You have all the tools and resources you need to begin building financial security

(2)

REWRITING YOUR MONEY STORY

The early memories of money from childhood can often dictate your adult relationship with money. Some of my earliest memories of money came from listening to my parents' conversations and realizing money was a source of stress for them. However, subconsciously, it became a source of stress for me, too. Those thoughts stayed with me, and I carried the fear of running out of money into my adulthood for a long time. Even though I was aware these are irrational fears, they're rooted in years of a scarcity mindset that I've begun to undo in my adult life.

Take a moment to think about your first memory of money. Maybe you feel excitement, anxiety, or even fear. Were you taught that money is hard to come by, it's impolite to talk about finances, or somewhere in between? Whatever the case, these beliefs can significantly affect your relationship with money now and into the future.

The good news is that financial behaviors and mindsets can be changed if you approach the topic with a growth mindset. In this chapter, we'll unravel your subconscious beliefs and emotions about money and explore how to shift from a scarcity mindset to one of abundance, helping you create the life you want.

WHAT ARE MONEY BELIEFS?

Money beliefs are attitudes and assumptions that subconsciously affect your financial decision-making. They are usually shaped by your experiences, upbringing, and the cultural or societal environment you grew up in. For example, if you were raised in a family that believed money is hard to come by, you might think that money is something to be hoarded for security. Alternatively, if you were taught that money comes and goes quickly, maybe you're more casual about it, assuming there's always more to be made.

These subconscious beliefs can significantly affect the financial decisions you make daily, whether that's how much you spend, how much you save, or even whether you invest for the future. Your money beliefs can also affect how you feel about money, whether you see it as a source of stress or a tool for empowerment.

Moreover, money beliefs can limit or expand what you think is financially possible. For instance, someone with a scarcity mindset might believe they'll never achieve financial success, while someone with an abundance mindset might be more confident in their ability to grow wealth.

COMMON BELIEFS

Your money beliefs or preconceived notions about money are internalized from childhood. However, your money mindset can change over time, like a growth mindset. Let's debunk some common money beliefs.

#1: "It's Selfish to Want Money"

Many people grow up believing that wanting money or pursuing wealth is inherently selfish or greedy. This belief is often passed down from family and friends. You can even see this notion portrayed in TV shows or movies. But in reality, money is simply a medium that amplifies the type of person you naturally are. If you are kind and generous, those traits are magnified with more money. The same logic applies in reverse. It's not bad to want to build a secure future and wealth for you and your family. It's the most responsible thing you can do.

#2: "I'll Never Be Rich"

This belief stems from a scarcity mindset, where building wealth seems like an uphill battle and that only certain people can be "rich." Some people assume that being rich requires a privileged background. While that may be the case for some, many people have gone from modest beginnings to achieving financial success through discipline, smart choices, and persistence. Many "everyday millionaires" build their wealth over time by saving, investing, and advancing their careers. They make smart choices with what they have. It's entirely possible to rewrite your financial future by prioritizing and taking small actions daily toward your financial goals.

#3: "I'm Just Bad with Money"

This belief becomes a self-fulfilling prophecy for many. If you believe you're bad with money, you're less likely to try improving your financial situation, because you assume it's beyond your control. But the truth is, nobody is born magically knowing how to manage money—it is learned through experience and education. Mistakes are part of that learning process. For instance, maybe you've racked up credit card debt in the past, but that doesn't mean you're destined to be bad with money for the rest of your life. You can adopt new money habits as long as you commit to doing the inner work and prioritize your money goals..

#4: "Money Doesn't Grow on Trees"

While it's true that money isn't infinite, the belief that there's never enough can cause people to focus on lack instead of opportunity. If you grew up in a household where your parents constantly worried about paying bills, you might have the internalized belief that money is "limited" or rooted in scarcity. But there are enough opportunities in the world to go around for everyone. By shifting your mindset from scarcity to abundance, you'll recognize opportunities to grow your income through career growth, side hustles, or investing.

#5: "Spending Money Is Irresponsible"

Many people grow up equating spending money with irresponsibility. Perhaps they saw family members struggle financially or witnessed reckless spending that led to financial hardship. While it's true that careless spending can have negative consequences, spending itself isn't inherently bad. How and why you spend money is what matters. Buying things that enhance your quality of life or align with your values is part of a healthy financial plan and contributes to your happiness. For example, investing in experiences like travel or education brings wealth (such as experience and knowledge) that can't be equated with money. And that's just as important. The key is learning to differentiate between mindless spending and intentional spending.

Gen Z Reality Check

Due to the lack of financial literacy education in our schools and homes, some may inherit outdated beliefs about money without even realizing it. Social media can also cloud our judgment about money in subtle ways. Here's what my community shared about the beliefs they have formed about money.

"Growing up in an immigrant household, I was never taught basic financial literacy and viewed the topic of money in a negative light. I only learned this during university through peers and educational resources but still find budgeting and investing difficult as an early adult with 'adult money' now."

—Anna, 24 years old

"As I started my financial journey, I started to become aware of the fact that I reflected a lot of inherited financial fear from my parents. I never had enough, and managing finances brought up so much anxiety."

—Anamika, 22 years old

"I think the most challenging thing is fighting FOMO. I want to save money, but when I see people post, it makes me feel left out, so I [want] to spend in other ways."

—Sarahi, 18 years old

YOUR PAST IS PRESENT

Growing up in an Asian immigrant household, frugality was a core value and it manifested in various ways. Generally, my parents never bought new things unless the current thing they were using either broke or became utterly unusable. One of the biggest examples I remember is when my dad refused to update our 25-year-old car even when the engine started to fail. "Oh, don't worry, we'll just get it repaired!" he'd say. Spoiler alert: It eventually stopped working, and we had to get it towed. After starting my "big girl job" postgrad, I eventually replaced the car out of impatience and frustration! LOL.

I'm grateful for many of my family's experiences and lessons because they *positively* impacted my financial outlook and behaviors. They taught me valuable lessons about the importance of money and prioritizing long-term financial goals over short-term gratification. I learned not to spend unnecessarily and to appreciate saving for important things.

However, there are some downsides to this approach. I prioritized saving money above all else, which created an underlying feeling of scarcity—a sense that I never had enough, and that good things came only if I deprived myself.

Childhood is often the foundation of our financial habits. The lessons we internalize—positive or negative—shape how we handle money in adulthood. For example, financial instability in childhood can leave people feeling like they're always one paycheck away from disaster, even when they're financially secure later in life. This constant sense of financial insecurity often limits their willingness to take calculated risks, even when they have the resources to do so.

The more fortunate also experience the effects of beliefs about money from childhood. I know people who grew up in financially comfortable households. Yet, they were taught to be overly cautious, so spending money became something to worry about rather than enjoy. This kind of financial over-vigilance can lead to a belief that money is something to obsess over without ever enjoying it.

These examples show that your past influences your present behaviors and mindset. By being aware of how your upbringing has shaped your views on money, you can begin to set healthier boundaries around saving and spending.

SCARCITY VS. ABUNDANCE MINDSET

It's easy to fall into the trap of feeling like there's never enough—never enough money, success, or resources. I think it's important to take a closer look at the different mindsets people can have about money. Remember, a scarcity mindset is a belief that you have a limited amount of success, resources, or opportunities available. When you think this way, it's easy to think someone else's success somehow takes away from your own. This belief creates unnecessary pressure and reinforces feelings of lack.

Conversely, an "abundance mindset" is the belief that there's more than enough success, wealth, or happiness. Another person's win doesn't detract from your own potential. Adopting an abundance mindset allows you to focus on what you have and the opportunities available rather than fixating on what's missing. When you internalize the belief that opportunities are everywhere, your subconscious mind will work to begin to notice things you can do to reach your goals.

Seeing my parents fear they didn't have enough money made me internalize that fear, especially as I got older. Later, I realized this mindset wasn't productive; it held me back and prevented me from entirely focusing on the present and embracing new opportunities. However, shifting to an abundance mindset doesn't happen overnight. It takes intentional effort to train the mind to focus on possibilities instead of limitations, but embracing this is liberating.

Anna Breaks the Cycle of Financial Fear

Anna grew up in a low-income household where her parents emphasized that money was hard to come by. They always tried to save as much as they could. Even when her family's financial situation improved, Anna's parents held onto those beliefs. They were constantly concerned about preparing for future emergencies. At a young age, Anna internalized that money was scarce and unpredictable, carrying this mindset into adulthood. She tried to avoid non-essential spending and felt guilty when purchasing things she enjoyed, even when she could afford them.

As Anna entered her twenties and began earning a solid income (even more than her parents), she still worried about money—even when she logically knew she had the means and didn't need to. She constantly felt stuck when making investments or larger purchases, like buying a home.

Anna was open about her financial fears to her friends and therapist. Both helped her work through financial trauma and establish healthier money beliefs. One of the biggest lessons she realized was to search for more opportunities to increase her earning potential, like advocating for a promotion at work. She also planned to apply her existing skills to a business. Anna became more intentional with her spending. She prioritized buying experiences and things that brought her the most joy, allowing herself to enjoy the fruits of her hard work without feeling guilty.

WHAT'S YOUR MONEY STORY?

As you read this chapter, you may have started reflecting on your life story about money. Is it based on deeply internalized childhood beliefs or scripts from society at large?

Take some time to reflect on these questions to dig deeper into your money story. Feel free to write down your answers in a notebook or journal if that helps you explore your thoughts and feelings.

- When you think about spending money, what feelings come up? Excitement, guilt, fear, freedom, or anything else?

- How did your parents or family talk about money? Was it a source of tension or security in your household?

- Have you ever felt ashamed or proud of your financial situation? Why?

- What does financial success mean to you? Is it defined by a number, lifestyle, or sense of security?

Once you've reflected on these, list five key beliefs you currently hold about money below. They might sound like "Money is scarce and hard to earn," "Money gives me freedom," or even "I'm not good at managing money." Write these down without judgment, as they will offer valuable insight into how past experiences continue shaping your present financial behavior.

1. _____

   _____

   _____

2. _____

   _____

   _____

3. _____

   _____

   _____

4. _____

   _____

   _____

   _____

   _____

   _____

By identifying these core beliefs, you'll begin to understand the patterns behind your financial decisions and allow yourself to rewrite your money narrative. Whether it's oversaving out of fear or overspending to avoid difficult emotions, this awareness is the first step toward developing more mindful and intentional financial habits that align with your goals and values.

PUT IT INTO ACTION: REWRITING YOUR MONEY STORY

You've had the chance to reflect on your money beliefs. Some of your feelings toward money may be helping you reach your goals (think goals rooted in abundance), while others might be holding you back (think goals rooted in scarcity). The good news? Just because you've had certain beliefs about money for a long time doesn't mean you have to stick with them. Let's begin rewriting your internal money script.

Step 1: Take Another Look at Your Beliefs

First, go back to that list of five money beliefs you wrote down. Look at each one and ask yourself: Does this belief help me move forward, or is it keeping me stuck? Some of your beliefs might feel good, while others might bring up some not-so-great feelings. That's okay! This is just about figuring out which beliefs need a little rewriting.

For example, if you wrote down something like "Money is scarce and hard to earn," it's time to challenge that thought. Is this belief true, or is it based on internalized beliefs?

Step 2: Flip the Script

Now, it's time to reframe those limiting beliefs. If you believe money is scarce and hard to earn, change your belief to, "I can create opportunities to earn money and manage it wisely."

See how that feels? It opens up more possibilities and puts you in control.

Here are a few more examples to help you get started:

- "I'll never have enough to feel secure" becomes "I'm working toward financial security, and every little bit helps."

- "I can't afford to spend money on myself" becomes "It's okay to invest in myself, and I can do it responsibly."

The idea is to change the way you talk to yourself about money. When you flip those limiting beliefs, you see new possibilities and open up more opportunities to improve your financial life. For instance, by shifting your mindset to something like, "I can create ways to make money," you become open to new pathways for career and financial growth. These could include starting a side hustle, negotiating a raise, or investing in something that could pay off.

Use the following space to reframe any of your limiting beliefs.

1. _____

_____

2. _____

_____

3. _____

_____

4. _____

_____

5. _____

_____

Step 3: Build on Your Positive Beliefs

Now that you understand your beliefs about money, let's take a moment to build on them. For example, if you believe "Money gives me freedom," think about how you can make that even more accurate. Could you use your resources to invest in experiences that bring you joy or support causes that matter to you?

Step 4: Practice the New Script

The final step? Practice, practice, practice! Rewriting your money beliefs is great, but it's about ensuring these new beliefs become part of your daily life. For example, if you're trying to learn about personal finance and it feels difficult, shift your internal dialogue to "I can learn about and be good with money." The more you believe it, the more likely it'll become your reality.

When you face a financial decision, check in with yourself: Are you reverting to old habits or trying to approach it from a different perspective? Consciously considering this "new script" might initially feel weird, but it will eventually become more natural.

MISTAKES ARE YOUR TEACHERS

It's inevitable to make mistakes, especially on your financial journey. No matter how much you prepare, there will be moments
when things don't go as planned, and that's okay. Some of those
moments can be your greatest teachers.

A few years ago, I made the mistake of investing in a meme
coin, a type of cryptocurrency based on a popular internet meme.
My decision wasn't rooted in research; I based it purely on hype.
Lo and behold, I lost money (but luckily, only $50). I initially felt
foolish and frustrated at myself, but this experience taught me the
importance of doing my homework before making investment
decisions. Now, I always research thoroughly and understand what
I'm getting into before investing in something.

The key is to approach mistakes with a mindset of growth.
Instead of dwelling on what went wrong, ask yourself, "What can
I learn from this?" Whether you missed a bill payment or made
an impulsive investment, each mistake is an opportunity to gain
insight and become better with your money.

Think about a time when you made a financial mistake. What
did you learn from it, and how can you use it to make better choices moving forward?

The (True) Value of Money

"Money can't buy happiness" is a phrase we always hear. But is it true?

Yes and no. You might've heard of a famous study by Daniel Kahneman and Angus Deaton, professors at Princeton University and Nobel Prize laureates. They declared that happiness tops out at around $75,000 in annual income. But surprisingly (or not-so-surprisingly), a more recent study from the Proceedings of the National Academy of Sciences (PNAS) published in 2022 shows that money boosts happiness for most people, up to $500,000.

So, while studies give us one perspective, my personal experiences have shown me another aspect. I can't deny that money doesn't bring me happiness because having a roof over my head and food to eat *definitely* makes me happy. Money also helps make life more convenient—you can use it to buy back your time, quit a job you don't enjoy, help the people you care about, and a lot more. For instance, I've taken my family to travel to several countries abroad, which are some of my happiest memories. Watching my loved ones experience new cultures and bond together was priceless, something that money enabled but couldn't create independently.

However, money can only do so much. It solves a lot of life's problems. But it can't buy happiness within or in your relationships with others. The connections we make, the passions we pursue, and the moments we cherish often bring the most joy—things that money alone can't provide.

Money is often not what we desire most, but the life that comes from it. The key is to develop a healthy relationship with money. The right path forward is using money to invest in your goals, create memories, and help others.

TALKING OPENLY ABOUT FINANCES

Talking about money can feel awkward, like "the ick." At least, that's what it seems society wants you to think. Most of us were raised to believe it's one of those "off-limits" topics, like politics at the dinner table or your eccentric cousin's love life. But here's the thing: Keeping money talk hush-hush does us more harm than good. When we stay quiet about finances, we miss out on tips and insights that benefit not just us but everyone around us. Luckily, times are changing, and these days, Gen Z is breaking free from the old-fashioned taboos that make it embarrassing or impolite to talk honestly about money.

For many people, not researching or asking coworkers what they're getting paid might mean they're not getting paid their worth. There are many more resources online you can tap into to learn about what other people are making at their jobs. Here are some sites you should consider looking into:

- **BLS.gov (U.S. Bureau of Labor Statistics):** This is a website from the U.S. federal government that has salary ranges for various job titles.

- **Levels.fyi:** This is a self-reported salary and total compensation website primarily focused on the tech industry.

- **LinkedIn:** This is a popular job site, and they list the expected salary ranges for posted job listings.

- **Glassdoor:** This site has employee reviews and self-reported pay for general role titles and roles at specific companies.

It's also more common now to see everyday people sharing their money journeys online and on social media. It's a good reminder of how empowering it can be to share knowledge and tips instead of gatekeeping. Talking about money with friends, family, or partners can benefit everyone. You get to swap tips, learn from each other's experiences, and feel less alone in figuring it all out. Plus, it's a great way to make sure you're not getting left behind when it comes to salary, budgeting, or investing.

So, how do you start these conversations without it feeling awkward? Approach it with curiosity and an open mind. Maybe you start by sharing something you learned recently, like a money-saving hack or a budgeting app you've been trying out. When it comes to talking with your partner, make it a team effort. Set aside time to chat about your goals, be honest about your income and expenses, and figure out a plan together.

KNOW YOUR REAL WORTH

When I was at UC Berkeley, it was very common for people to ask, "Where are you interning this summer?" or "Where are you working after graduation?" This is *particularly true* among students in the business school that I attended. This is probably why everyone unofficially nicknamed the business students as "the snakes."

Thinking back on it, I now find that line of questioning fairly toxic. The pitfall of linking self-worth with net worth is that it creates a constant cycle of comparison. It sets you up to never be "enough" because there's always someone with a higher salary or a more prestigious job. This mindset can lead to stress, burnout, and even poor financial decisions.

Flipping this idea requires redefining success from the inside out. When we focus on improving our sense of self-worth—by building confidence in our abilities, aligning with our core values, and cultivating a life that feels meaningful—we often find that our net worth follows suit.

Start by setting goals that resonate with who you are rather than what others expect. Focus on skills, relationships, and activities that bring fulfillment outside of financial success. True self-worth leads to making choices that enhance our financial stability and success because they're rooted in our own values, not external validation.

TAKEAWAYS
THE NEW RULES OF YOUR MONEY STORY

We learn lessons about money from a young age, often without even realizing it. No matter what your relationship is with money, it's never too late to rewrite your story for the better.

OLD RULES	NEW RULES
Some people are born with the ability to be "good" with money and some people aren't	Your childhood experiences shape your relationship with money. You have the power to reshape it
When other people succeed, there's less opportunity for you	Focusing on what's possible opens more opportunities than worrying about what you lack
You have to be very hard on yourself to achieve financial success	Being kind to yourself and learning from your mistakes help to create a better relationship with money
It isn't polite to talk openly about money	Having open conversations about money can help you advocate for a higher income
Your net worth determines your self-worth	Define self-worth on your own terms to set yourself up for greater success

(3)

MAKING MONEY (AND BANKING IT)

It's time to get into the nitty-gritty! Your career and earning potential are the foundations of your personal finances. But when you're young, knowing if you're on the right path with your work and finances can be confusing.

If you're still figuring out your career options, this chapter will help you explore matching your interests and strengths with a viable career path. If you're already in your chosen field, you'll find tips on getting ahead and advocating for promotions and raises.

I'll also discuss the basics of banking your earnings, paying your taxes, and building an emergency fund to protect against life's curveballs. Let's dive in!

YOUR EARNINGS

When you're young, you have a lot of time but not a ton of money; when you're older, you have more money but less time. When you're young, time is your most valuable asset because once you spend it, there's no getting it back. I believe it's important to balance enjoying yourself in the present and saving for the future. Plus, when you have time, you can explore your interests and figure out what you like doing (career-wise or personal interests).

Your twenties are for figuring out your career interests and paving a strong path to set yourself up for a higher earning potential as you get more established in the workforce. It can be challenging when you are new to work culture. I view it as learning a different language, especially if you've spent most of your life in school. Besides the work, you might be experiencing other big "adulting" changes, like finding a place to rent, navigating a new city, learning how to manage your earnings, and many other things.

Maybe you're navigating an hourly wage job or taking on your first salaried role. Both paths are valuable stepping stones. Hourly jobs offer flexibility and opportunities to build foundational skills, while salaried roles provide stability and a chance to gain deeper industry experience. It's important to look for opportunities so that you keep learning new skills, being proactive, and growing as a person.

It's normal to feel like you're not earning as much as you'd like in your twenties, but remember, this is a period of growth and investment in yourself! The more you learn, the more valuable you become as an employee or entrepreneur, which translates into higher earnings down the road.

Gen Z Reality Check

When it comes to making enough money to start saving, Gen Z is finding things, well, challenging. What we earn doesn't stretch as far as we would like. However, with online shopping and targeted advertising, spending what we have is easier than ever. Here's what my community had to say about making money in the world today.

> "The current salary range is insufficient to cover basic living expenses, including utilities, groceries, and essential needs. It leaves little to no room for saving."
>
> —Rokaya, 23 years old

> "Earning money feels like a constant uphill battle, but spending it is just a click away. We're constantly bombarded with ads and trends, making it hard to resist the urge to buy things we don't need, [which] leads to financial instability."
>
> —Angelica, 23 years old

> "Personal finance wasn't even on my radar [in college], but now it feels like an essential skill I need to catch up on to be successful... It helps to find people who are at a similar stage, as well as those who are a few steps ahead, and pull bits and pieces from their experiences to create a plan that works for me."
>
> —Aleksina, 22 years old

YOUR CAREER PATH

A career path is rarely linear. For most people, it's like a roller coaster, with unpredictable twists and turns. Ideally, the path you take should align with your interests while having a level of market demand. In this section, we'll discuss how to explore your interests when figuring out your career path and give tips if you're already in your chosen field.

IF YOU'RE STILL FIGURING OUT YOUR CAREER PATH

"The world is your oyster." You've heard this one before, right? Young people are often told this timeless phrase to let them know they can do what they wish and go where they want.

While this statement can feel freeing, it can also cause you to experience analysis paralysis because of all the possibilities. You may have an inkling of what you want to do or have no idea. The good news is that time is on your side to explore your interests more deeply.

Here are a few questions to help you clarify your career path. Reflecting on your career path can help you understand what you enjoy doing and where your strengths lie.

- What sorts of activities did you enjoy when you were younger?

- What were your favorite subject(s) in school?

- What do you enjoy spending your free time doing?

- What sorts of advice do your friends come to you for?

- What are your biggest strengths?

- What topic(s) could you talk about for hours without getting bored?

- Which achievements are you most proud of and why?

Gaining insight into your interests and strengths can help you figure out what job you can align them with. We live in a capitalistic society, so if you want to enjoy financial security, your career path should have market demand. This means that some people or organizations need the skills you're offering *and* are willing to pay for your services. This is true whether you are an employee or a business owner. It can take some time to figure out the right career path, so don't worry if it isn't clear to you yet.

Exploring Your Career Options

Full-time employment is where you work 40 hours a week and your salary is fixed; hourly employees are considered full time if they are guaranteed 40 hours per week. Full-time employment typically comes with health insurance (which, in the U.S., is often tied to employment), paid time off, and retirement plan contributions. However, part-time, seasonal and contract work, internships, and apprenticeships are also possible. If you're still figuring things out, and have the financial ability to do so, consider starting with internships or part-time roles to test different fields without committing to full-time.

If you're considering college or higher education to improve your career outcomes, you might wonder: Is college worth it anymore? I'm here to say yes. Generally, higher education opens up your career options. Typical earnings for someone with a bachelor's degree are 86% higher than those with only a high school diploma.

If you choose the college route, it's important to get a return on investment, as your earnings after graduation should surpass what you paid for your education. I encourage you to work backward by researching roles you're interested in, looking at their average pay, and identifying the majors that qualify you for these jobs. Crunch the numbers to figure out if the career you want to go into can outpace the cost of the degree.

Remember, there are many educational options to consider. These include two-year associate degrees and four-year bachelor's degrees. Other paths like vocational or trade schools are also good options. In fact, these types of schools offer quicker, more affordable paths to a stable and well-paying career. Careers like electricians, plumbers, or dental hygienists are in high demand, often provide competitive salaries, and don't require a four-year degree. These careers can provide financial security while bypassing the student debt associated with traditional colleges.

You can also explore certifications, boot camps, or online courses in growing fields like data analysis or user experience (UX) and user interface (UI) design. These paths allow you to gain in-demand skills in a shorter time frame without the significant financial commitment of a full degree. By researching what skills are in demand and what you enjoy doing, you can make an informed decision on whether college, a trade program, or self-study is the right route for you. It also helps to talk to professionals in your desired fields, read job descriptions, or use resources like the Occupational Outlook Handbook (BLS.gov/ooh).

Turning Internships into Career Gold

These days, it's not uncommon to see entry-level jobs require one to three years of prior experience. Ironic, right? Hands down, one of the best ways to gain experience, especially if you are a college student, is to apply for internships. They're basically like short-term jobs companies provide to help students get real-life work experience in their field of interest. Internships can range from 1 month to 12 months, but summer internships are most common, which could last 2 to 3 months. Most internships are short-term and are a great, low-risk way to explore different career interests while trying out different fields to see what you can do after graduation.

When I was in college, I knew I wanted to pursue a career in the business and tech fields, so I was open to trying and learning many things. In the summer of my freshman year, I interned at a small consulting firm, which helped me learn about working in a company environment. Plus, it gave me some experience to put on my resume for the following recruiting cycles. In the summer of my sophomore year, I interned at a tech startup, where I learned more about marketing and sales while building my resume even more.

In the spring of my junior year, I took on a longer internship with a bigger tech startup. That experience was super eye-opening—I got to see firsthand how things work at a larger company. This experience enabled me to land an internship at one of the most impactful tech companies in the world in the summer of my junior year at college. They had a formal internship program with tons of other university interns—mentorship, learning programs, community building, etc. It was the best internship by far, and I learned so much in such a short period of time.

Top Tips for Internships

Here are some key tips if you decide to go down the internship route:

Start earlier rather than later. By going through this process multiple times, I've been able to practice my interview skills, which, over time, helped me feel prepared when it came to applying for some of the internships that I really wanted. The other approach is applying to internships as early as you can before the following summer. Many companies will open their internship programs for the summer ten months in advance. This means that you have to start applying for some of these internships in the fall semester before the year the internship actually starts. If the lead time on an internship is close to a year out, it's likely that the company and role are in demand, so expect a lot of competition.

Make the most of online sites. You can search for internships on sites like LinkedIn (linkedin.com) and Indeed (indeed.com). Handshake (joinhandshake.com) is a site tailored specifically toward college students and recent grads (<5 years of work experience) that features a community of recruiters and company events alongside job postings. This platform came in clutch for me so many times. I've attended a lot of on-campus recruiting events, many of which I found through Handshake, where representatives from various companies would come to my school. It's a great way to meet industry professionals. Alternatively, you can also go directly to the web pages of companies you are interested in to look for and apply for internships. This can help make sure your application goes straight to the hiring manager without any third-party vetting.

Get a referral to a company if you can. Depending on the industry and company, getting a referral from a current employee can help your resume get noticed more easily and increase your chances of getting an interview for an internship. But it's also not the end of the world if you can't get a referral. I've gotten a decent number of interviews just by applying cold on a company website.

Apply to as many internships as possible. Landing an internship is a numbers game. I applied to close to a thousand internships throughout my time in college and ended up with a handful of offers. To my resume, I added relevant coursework as well as activities I did in college (e.g., school clubs, leadership positions, personal projects). I also tweaked my resume bullet points slightly to tailor my resume depending on the job role. It can be a lot if you hear rejections from internships you applied to (or if they ghost your application completely), but don't take it too personally. You only need one yes! Don't put all your eggs in one basket, and be open-minded about opportunities that come your way.

Make an impression to land a job. Here's an internship hack that's not widely discussed: Many medium- to large-sized companies will hire new grads straight from their internship programs. I speak from personal experience: After completing and performing well during my junior summer internship, I received a full-time offer at the start of my senior year to return to the same company after graduation.

PUT IT INTO ACTION:
FIND YOUR PURPOSE WITH *IKIGAI*

If you're still on the path to figuring out what you want to do career-wise, I want to introduce you to the Japanese concept of **ikigai**. Essentially, ikigai means finding a purpose that brings you joy in life. It combines four important categories: what you love, what you are good at, what you can be paid for, and what the world needs. The intersection of these four categories forms your ikigai. It is helpful to think about, whether you're looking at what kinds of job you want or you're looking to start a business and need to figure out what you want to offer!

Here's an example of what ikigai looks like for me. By combining what I enjoy and am good at with what I can be paid for and what the world needs, I've found a fulfilling career in marketing and teaching others about professional development and financial literacy.

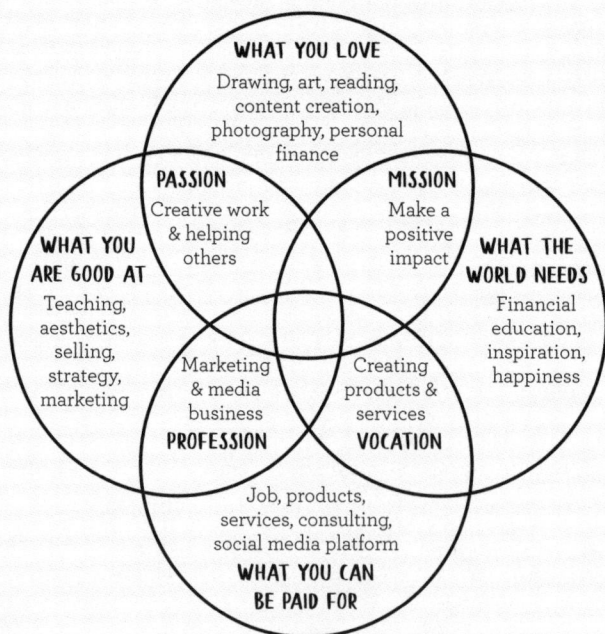

WHAT YOU LOVE
Drawing, art, reading, content creation, photography, personal finance

PASSION
Creative work & helping others

MISSION
Make a positive impact

WHAT YOU ARE GOOD AT
Teaching, aesthetics, selling, strategy, marketing

WHAT THE WORLD NEEDS
Financial education, inspiration, happiness

Marketing & media business
PROFESSION

Creating products & services
VOCATION

Job, products, services, consulting, social media platform
WHAT YOU CAN BE PAID FOR

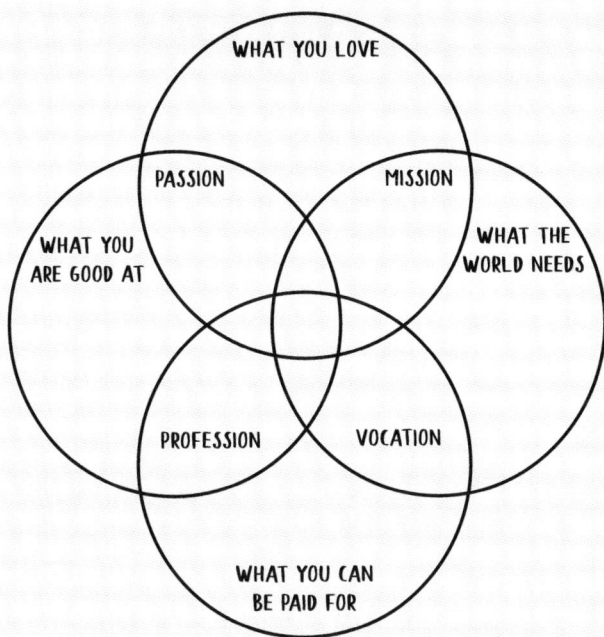

Here is a blank version of the ikigai diagram. I encourage you to use the space to brainstorm and jot down your thoughts for each of the sections to help you gain more clarity on your passions and interests, and how these intersect with what the world needs. There's no right or wrong way to approach this—some of you might walk away with a clear, singular ikigai where your passions, talents, and earning potential perfectly intersect. However, it's also okay if you end up with more than one possible ikigai or if your main focus is on singular elements, like your profession.

After completing the diagram, take a moment to identify one small action you can take toward aligning with your ikigai. For example, if you realize you love teaching, you might explore tutoring opportunities or start creating educational content online. The key is to take that first step, no matter how small, toward living a life aligned with your purpose.

Making Extra Cash with a Side Hustle

As a certified side hustler since childhood, I'm a big proponent of finding creative ways to make extra money outside your main income. I started creating content on social media in college out of boredom and as a fun outlet to share my experiences. It's one of the best decisions I've made, both from a career and a personal growth perspective. It has allowed me to have more breathing room in my finances to beef up my savings and to take my parents traveling to places we've never been!

If you're looking for quick, consistent cash, you might consider:

- **Surveys or focus groups:** These are easy to sign up to online and fit in during downtime.

- **Deliveries:** Apps like DoorDash or Uber Eats offer flexible hours.

- **Babysitting or pet sitting:** Great for evenings or weekends.

- **Tutoring:** Use your skills to help others in subjects you excel at.

- **Freelance work:** From writing to graphic design, you can leverage your talents online.

If you're aiming for something with more growth potential and something that could become a longer-term business, think about projects that allow you can leverage your skills or passions. You might consider:

- **Selling handmade goods:** Platforms like Etsy make it easy to reach customers.

- **Consulting:** Provide professional advice in your area of expertise. You can do this by offering your services on websites like Fiverr and UpWork or build a professional website to showcase your past work to attract clients.

- **Content creation:** Share your knowledge or hobbies on YouTube, TikTok, or Instagram while building an audience and brand.

Your side hustle might open the door to big opportunities and eventually replace your main source of income.

Interestingly, Gen Z leads the way with side hustles. Nearly half of us engage in one (a higher rate than earlier generations). Still, it's important to note that if you are content with your main job and have a fulfilling life outside of it, it's okay not to pursue a side hustle! It comes down to your priorities and what you want to get out of starting a side gig.

IF YOU'RE ALREADY IN YOUR CHOSEN FIELD

If you are lucky enough to already know what field you want to go into or you are already in it, you may be thinking about how to take your next steps. Let's look at some useful advice.

One of the most important concepts I've learned when it comes to a career is the idea of "your network is your net worth." This includes building relationships with a trusted group of mentors and advocates in your field. Think of this as your "personal board of directors" that can help guide you to where you want to go. When I was a college student, I learned so much about specific career paths and advice from mentors and peers, as well as alumni who were a few years ahead of me. This idea also includes building relationships at your company or field of work, so you'd have people who become familiar with your work and advocate for your growth.

Growing up, I was taught that my work would speak for itself. "As long as you work hard, your achievements will be recognized" is something my family always told me. Well, I'm here to say that's not completely true. Having people that back up and support you is equally important because so many doors are opened by people.

Aside from relationship building, it's also important to continuously learn and advance your skills, whether that's through books, classes, training programs, certifications, or more. I'm a big believer that learning doesn't stop when you finish school.

Focus on creating value and impact, not just making money. Yes, money is important, but it's typically a byproduct of the value you provide to organizations and people. The more value you're able to provide, the more money you will receive. Think about learning high-income skills, providing a product or service that will help other people, and more.

Finally, at your job, you should be either learning or earning (both in an ideal world). If it's neither, it might be worth considering a new job or role.

PROMOTIONS AND RAISES

Promotions and raises are key areas to consider when growing your career—I mean, who doesn't wanna be paid more?

When it comes to work, it's still a common theory to work with your head down and to "let your work speak for itself." Unfortunately, I learned that hard work by itself isn't enough. When I started my first job after graduating from college, I noticed that the people who got the promotions were not the ones who worked the hardest. Instead, they excelled at marketing their work to everyone around them and promoting their image to their teams and bosses. An example would be to send out an email with key accomplishments to any teams you work with when you successfully complete a project or include a few slides about a recent project you led at the next team meeting.

Truth be told, the thing standing between you and what you want—whether it's a new job, a promotion, or a raise—is other people. People often complicate things by thinking there's this grand system that makes decisions, but most of the time, your fate is in the hands of others. Remember, the people who make promotion decisions have thoughts and feelings. Their decisions can be driven by irrationality even when presented with facts and logic. This simplifies things a lot—most things we do depend on building and maintaining (positive) relationships with other people. For instance, a manager at work may promote someone they like, not the one who is qualified.

I'm thankful that I realized this early on. After getting a sense of how things worked in my first job, I focused on building relationships with the people I worked with, whether my direct team or cross-functional teams I worked closely with. I met mentors with whom I clicked and asked how to navigate the company culture, and which useful skills were most needed to succeed in the job. I walked away with snippets of information for personal and professional growth that would've taken me longer to learn on my own.

Every time I finished a large project, I made sure to send a recap of the results and impact to leadership teams and relevant company members. The key is to make yourself visible and leave a trail of evidence of your work, showing how your work benefited the organization. I also recommend keeping a running document of things you've done with the results or impact of your work and screenshots of praise you receive from coworkers.

During my first promotion cycle, about two years after starting this job, I presented the facts of my case—a list of specific projects I worked on, the impact of my work, and the praise I received from my colleagues—to demonstrate my positive performance and provide evidence that I was qualified to move up a rung on the ladder.

Remember, closed mouths don't get fed. The great thing about Gen Z is that we're much more vocal about promotions and pay raises than older generations! As much as I wish to believe that others are always looking out for you, no one will care as much about your career as you do. It almost never hurts to ask about an upcoming promotion or pay raise, because the worst thing that your boss can say is no. Don't wait for others to give you permission. Instead, take matters into your own hands.

Standing Up for Yourself

No one deserves to be underpaid or treated unfairly at work. It's important to know that fairness isn't just about recognition—it's about making sure you're getting what you're legally entitled to.

If you ever feel like something's off with your pay or treatment, the first thing to do is understand your rights. In the U.S., laws like the **Fair Labor Standards Act (FLSA)** provide protection to workers about minimum wage and overtime pay. You'll also want to check out your state's labor laws, as they can sometimes offer even more protections.

A good habit is to keep track of your hours worked (if you're in an hourly position), projects completed, and any feedback or praise you receive. This way, if you need to raise an issue, you've got the receipts. Start by chatting with your HR team or taking a look at your employee handbook to see what your company says about pay and treatment.

If you don't get anywhere internally, outside resources can help. The **U.S. Department of Labor** (website: DOL .gov) is a good starting point, and some nonprofits offer free or low-cost legal advice. If you're in a union, that's another useful option. And remember, some laws protect you from getting in trouble for speaking up—so don't hesitate to ask questions.

Bottom line: Your job should be a place where you feel valued and respected. If something doesn't feel right, it's okay to stand up for yourself and ask for what you deserve.

LET'S TALK TAXES

You can't talk about money without talking about taxes. They are the biggest line items you'll pay each year. Ah, the reward of making money. If the thought of paying taxes freaks you out, I have a useful approach for you to consider. Imagine you bake a pie, and that pie represents your total income for the year. However, you don't get to keep the whole pie to yourself because Uncle Sam (the government) will always take his slice. Here's how your pie breaks down:

Federal income taxes: The government takes a big slice to help pay for things like public services and national defense. Federal income tax brackets fall between 10% to 37%, as of 2025. The tax system in the U.S. is progressive, meaning that the more money you make, the bigger the slice they'll take.

State income taxes: Depending on where you live, your state might take a slice too, which can range from 0% to 13.3%. This goes toward state-level things like education, infrastructure, and healthcare.

Payroll taxes: These are slices that go toward specific programs like Social Security and Medicare, which help support people in retirement or in need of medical care. Payroll taxes are typically 7.65% of your income, with 6.2% to Social Security (up to a certain income cap) and 1.45% for Medicare.

Local taxes: Some cities or counties (but not all) will also take a smaller slice for things like local schools, libraries, or emergency services. Local taxes can fall between 0% to 3%.

Other taxes: If you buy certain things, like a house or a car, or even just shop at the store, sales taxes (generally ranging from 4% to 10%) and property taxes (1% to 2% or more of the property's assessed value) are additional smaller slices that can come out of your pie, too.

WHAT'S UP WITH TAX RATES?

A big misconception about taxes, at least in the U.S., is that it's not good to make too much money because you'll get taxed more. That is true—to an extent. But when you look at the entire picture around taxation in the U.S., you begin to see that statement is more of a myth than reality. The U.S. uses a system based on **marginal tax rates**, which means different chunks of your income are taxed at different rates. Think of it as a staircase. Each step represents a different tax rate. You start at the lowest rate and only move up to the next one for income that exceeds the previous step.

Here are the federal income tax brackets for single filers in 2025 (make sure to check with official sources as this can change annually):

TAX RATE	TAXABLE INCOME BRACKETS FOR SINGLE FILERS
10%	$0–$11,925
12%	$11,926–$48,475
22%	$48,476–$103,350
24%	$103,351–$197,300
32%	$197,301–$250,525
35%	$250,526–$626,350
37%	$626,351 and up

Still confused? (Don't worry, taxes *are* confusing at first.) Follow along!

Let's say you make $60,000 in 2025. Your tax rates would break down like this.

Taxable Income: $60,000

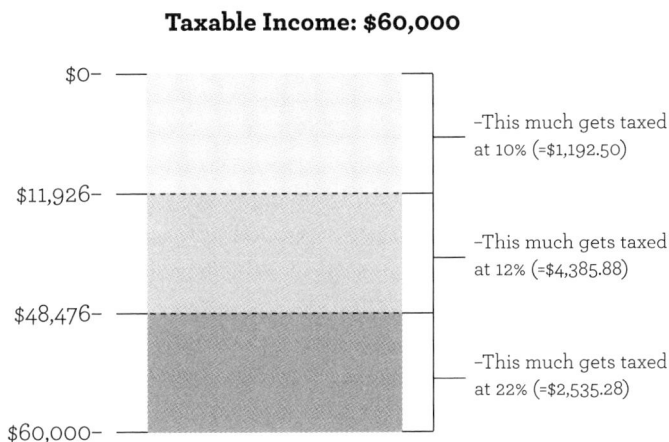

$0–	–This much gets taxed at 10% (=$1,192.50)
$11,926–	–This much gets taxed at 12% (=$4,385.88)
$48,476–	–This much gets taxed at 22% (=$2,535.28)
$60,000–	

Put simply, you don't pay the 22% rate on the entire $60,000, which would be $12,000. Instead, a marginal tax rate means you only pay $8,113.66 in taxes.

Your filing status also plays a role in your tax rates. Are you single or married? You can file taxes as Single, Head of Household, Married Filing Jointly, Married Filing Separately, or Qualified Surviving Spouse. The filing status that saves you the most money is Married Filing Jointly (the catch here is that you need to be married). If you're unsure of your status, you can take the quick quiz "What is my filing status?" at IRS.gov/help/ita/what-is-my-filing-status.

A shower thought: The next time you're about to spend money on something, think of it as paying with "after-tax dollars." So, if you buy something that is $100, it likely took you $125 worth of your time, energy, and hard work in order to buy that thing. Ask yourself, "Is this worth not just the dollars, but the energy and time it cost to earn those dollars?"

WHAT'S A W-4 FORM?

When you start a job, you'll typically have to submit a **W-4 form**. It's basically a way to let your employer know how much tax to take out of your paycheck. It helps make sure you're paying the right amount throughout the year, so you don't get hit with a big surprise tax bill or a massive refund when you file.

You'll fill out a W-4 when you start a new job or after a big life change—like getting married or having kids. The form asks about your filing status, dependents, and if you want any extra money withheld. It's especially useful if you have more than one job so you aren't hit with a big tax bill during tax season. You can also make adjustments if you've got other income or deductions. If you don't fill it out, your employer will assume you're single with no dependents and withhold more tax.

SAVE MONEY WITH TAX BREAKS

Taxes don't have to take as big a bite out of your income pie as it may seem at first glance. There are strategies to reduce your taxable income (which lowers the amount you owe) or qualify for tax credits (which directly reduce your tax bill). Here are some strategies to help you maximize tax breaks and keep more of your hard-earned money:

- **Contribute to Tax-Advantaged Retirement Accounts.** By contributing to accounts like a 401(k) or Traditional IRA (we'll look at these more in Chapter 6), you're essentially reducing your taxable income for the year. For example, if you make $50,000 and contribute $5,000 to your 401(k), you'll only be taxed on $45,000.

- **Use a Health Savings Account (HSA).** If you have a high-deductible health plan (HDHP), contributing to an HSA can give you a triple tax benefit: Contributions are tax-deductible, the money grows tax-free, and withdrawals used for qualified medical expenses are also tax-free. You can contribute up to $4,300 (individual) or $8,550 (family) in 2025. (We'll also look more at these in Chapter 6.)

- **Claim Credits.** Tax credits reduce your tax bill dollar-for-dollar, which is even better than a deduction. Some common tax credits include:

- **Earned Income Tax Credit (EITC):** For low-to-moderate income earners, the EITC can reduce your taxes and even result in a refund.

- **Lifetime Learning Credit (LLC):** If you or your dependents are pursuing higher education, this credit can provide up to $2,000 toward tuition and related expenses.

- **Business Deductions:** If you're self-employed, you can deduct business-related expenses like office supplies, travel, and even part of your home office if you use it exclusively for work. This reduces your taxable income and can save you big on taxes. Just make sure to keep receipts and documentation for all deductible expenses.

In terms of actually filing your taxes, it can be done online, using tax software like TurboTax or H&R Block. If your finances are more complicated, consider hiring an accountant. Don't forget taxes are usually due by April 15 each year. Filing late can result in penalties, so it's always better to file on time.

Sakura Manages "Adult Money" for the First Time

Sakura is a 22-year-old recent college grad who's excited to finally be earning "adult money" at her first job, at a consulting firm. Upon receiving her first paycheck, she realized she didn't understand how her paycheck was getting taxed. On top of learning how to manage her living expenses while getting settled in New York City, the thought of figuring out how to save and invest for the future overwhelmed her.

Sakura's first step was reviewing her paycheck breakdown and understanding how taxes work. She learned about the W-4 form she filled out when she started her job and how withholding impacts her paycheck. She also did research on how the U.S. tax system works and how much was being taken out for federal, state, and local taxes. (NYC has a city income tax for residents on top of NY state tax.) Sakura also prioritized putting a percentage of her income into a 401(k) retirement plan, which helps her lower her taxable income while also saving for her future.

Simultaneously, Sakura learned about which bank accounts she should open. She uses a checking account for her direct deposits from her job and for her daily spending. She was actually just leaving her money piled up in this checking out until she came across a video on her Instagram feed talking about high-yield savings accounts and realized she could be making some passive income (interest income in this case) by transferring some of her savings into a HYSA. It took her less than ten minutes to set up a HYSA and to get the ball rolling.

These are some good first steps when it comes to managing your income for the first time. We'll dive deeper into more strategies in the following chapters.

SETTING UP AN EMERGENCY FUND

Even if you attempt to plan out your life, things will happen that you don't anticipate. You get laid off, a sudden medical expense comes up, or your cat needs emergency surgery; the list can go on.

I've been wearing retainers since I was 11 years old. I got them after my braces were removed (I was an early bloomer in the teeth game). And let me tell you, I was diligent, wearing them every single night like clockwork. That is, until one time during a trip, I accidentally wrapped my retainer in a napkin at a restaurant (a rookie mistake, I know) and, of course, forgot all about it. By the time I realized what had happened, it was already long gone— probably in a dumpster somewhere.

Cue a $500 emergency orthodontist visit to replace the lost retainer. It wasn't something I had planned for, but this is exactly why having an **emergency fund** matters. An emergency fund helps you cover those unexpected expenses that come up while offering peace of mind. Having a financial cushion means you won't have to scramble for quick cash or swipe into credit card debt when life throws a surprise your way. Let's face it: Even the most careful among us can't always predict life's curveballs. And that's just the smaller stuff. Bigger emergencies, like a job loss or an unexpected medical bill, can put a much larger dent in your finances.

HOW MUCH SHOULD YOU SAVE?

So, how much should you aim for in your emergency fund? Ideally, you'll want to have three to six months' worth of living expenses set aside. It could even be for a longer duration, depending on what will help you sleep well at night. Start by figuring out your basic monthly expenses, like rent, groceries, transportation, and bills. Then, multiply that by the number of months you'd like your emergency fund to cover. Let's say your monthly expenses are $3,000, so you'll want to aim for at least $9,000 for a three-month cushion.

Starting an emergency fund can feel like a lofty goal, especially if you are starting from scratch or you're dealing with tight finances. But as mentioned previously, the key is to break a big goal into smaller goals. For instance, aim to save $1,000 first and gradually move the goalpost to reach the three- to six-months recommended threshold. Every little bit helps. When it comes to saving, treat your emergency funds like a bill you owe each month. That way, "paying yourself first" becomes part of your routine, just like rent or utilities.

Ideally, you'll want to park these funds in a high-yield savings account where it can earn some interest while staying easily accessible. (Don't worry, I'll explain more about choosing the right savings account on page 63.) For now, just know that it's important to keep the money separate from your everyday checking account so that you're not tempted to dip into it for non-emergencies.

BANKING BASICS

Just a few decades ago, banking was done IRL at your local branch with physical money, checkbooks, and paper forms. Thankfully, the rise of digital banking means you can now manage your money with a smartphone from the comfort of your couch. But there are still some banking basics to wrap your head around if you're new to the game.

CHOOSING A BANK ACCOUNT

Even though online banking has made it easier to manage money, you still need to know about the main types of bank accounts. Here's the rundown of the main types:

Checking Account: This is what most people typically think of when they hear "bank account." It's where your paychecks or pay usually get deposited into. Most people think of the big banks in this scenario: JPMorgan Chase, Bank of America, Citi, and Wells Fargo. Big national banks like these offer a ton of financial products, including savings accounts. However, the standard interest rate or annual percentage yield (APY), which describes the effective rate of return, at national banks is horrendous, around 0.01%. It's good to keep a small amount in your checking account for your bills and spending, but it is *not* a good place to put your savings or emergency funds.

High-Yield Savings Account (HYSA): A HYSA is a great place to park savings like an emergency fund. These offer an APY of around 2–5%, which is a *huge* jump from the APY offered by checking accounts. It's much higher because HYSAs typically operate from online-only banks. Think Marcus by Goldman Sachs, SoFi, Ally Bank, and many more, which became popular in the 2010s. The APY percentage changes depending on how the economy is doing and is largely due to interest rates set by the Federal Reserve, or the Feds. (They're best described as the big boss of the

U.S. economy.) For comparison, if you put $10,000 in a checking account with a 0.01% APY, you would earn a whopping $1 in interest in a year (boo!). If you put the same amount in a HYSA with a 4% APY, you would earn $400 in interest in a year (yay!). Note: This is a simplified example that doesn't take compounding into account. Most HYSAs are compounded daily (though some may compound less frequently), so the true interest amounts would be slightly higher depending on the compounding terms you use.

Money Market Account: This is similar to a savings account but usually requires a higher minimum balance, typically $1,000 or more. They can have higher APYs than traditional savings accounts but typically lower than HYSAs.

Certificate of Deposit (CD): This account locks your money for a set period in exchange for a fixed interest rate. While the interest can be higher than a HYSA, you lose flexibility since you can't access your money without penalties until the term ends.

"Okay, Lillian, but why would banks just give me money by parking my savings in there?" The answer to this lies in how the banking system works. When you put your money in a bank, it is able to lend your money out to consumers, businesses, and the government through loans, mortgages, or credit cards. The underlying principle is that the bank is able to loan out the money at a higher interest rate than what they're paying you. The difference between what they charge and what they pay is how banks make profits. By offering you interest on your savings, they're incentivizing you to keep your money in the bank; then they can lend out to others.

When choosing a bank account, consider factors like:

- **APY rates:** For savings, look for competitive interest rates like those from online HYSAs.

- **Fees:** Some accounts charge monthly maintenance fees or ATM fees—watch out for these.

- **Accessibility:** Is there a user-friendly mobile app? Are there physical branches if needed?

- **FDIC Insurance:** Make sure the bank is insured by the FDIC, meaning your money is protected up to $250,000 per depositor, per bank.

AVOIDING OVERDRAFTS

When it comes to buying things, be careful not to spend more than what's available in your account or you'll likely incur overdrafts. They can be costly—around $35 per transaction. To avoid these fees, consider these tips:

- **Overdraft protection:** Some banks offer protection by transferring money from your savings account to cover the shortfall, but this might still come with a small fee.

- **Linked accounts:** You can link your checking account to a savings or credit account to cover overdrafts with fewer fees.

- **Opt-out:** If you don't have enough funds, opt out of overdraft services to have transactions declined. This avoids fees, but it could lead to declined purchases.

- **Balance alerts:** Set up notifications to warn you when your balance is low, helping you avoid overdraft payments altogether.

- **Check your bank balance regularly:** Consider keeping a set amount in your checking account and check it regularly (at least once a week—put a reminder on your phone). This way you can ensure that your account balance doesn't go below a certain amount, and you can avoid the chance of an overdraft altogether.

JOINT VS. SEPARATE ACCOUNTS

A big question that comes up for those in relationships is whether you should combine finances into a **joint account** or keep them in **separate accounts**. Here's a quick guide to the pros and cons of each:

	PROS	CONS
Joint accounts	Easier for managing shared expenses Financial transparency Simplifying savings for joint goals	Less individual control over spending Potential disagreements about how the money is used
Separate accounts	Maintains financial independence Reduces arguments about personal spending	Managing shared expenses can be more complicated Less financial transparency

Many couples combine both approaches—using a joint account for shared bills and separate accounts for personal spending. This is a balance that provides convenience for shared goals while maintaining your financial independence. I strongly encourage women in relationships to have their own money that is not tied to their partner. It's so important to have access to your own funds so you have the freedom to make independent choices.

Every couple handles their finances differently, but communication is key: Talk about your financial goals and decide what works best for your relationship.

TAKEAWAYS

THE NEW RULES OF MAKING MONEY

Young people today may not have the job security that previous generations enjoyed, but this doesn't have to hold you back when it comes to advancing your career.

OLD RULES	NEW RULES
If you haven't figured out your career path in your twenties, you never will	Embrace your twenties as a time of learning and growth as you explore your career options
Stay loyal to the same employer to build your career	Changing jobs can help you secure a higher income and grow your career
Internships are just a way to build out your resume	Internships can lead to job offers if you make the right impression
Let your work speak for itself	Make yourself visible at work and document your success
Employers should begin conversations about promotions and raises	No one will care about your career as much as you do, so don't be afraid to advocate for a promotion or raise

(4)

LEVELING UP YOUR BUDGETING

Ah, budgeting—everyone's favorite topic, right? Okay, I know the idea of creating a budget doesn't bring to mind fun and excitement, but I promise it doesn't have to be as daunting as it seems.

If you've never made a budget before, it can be confusing as to where to start. And for many people, if not most, the concept of budgeting can feel restrictive. But here's the truth: A budget isn't meant to restrict or limit you. Knowing where your money is going can help you feel more in control of your finances, whether you've just scored your first part-time job or are earning a yearly salary. No matter at what stage you are in your career or finances, budgeting is important in order to maintain this sense of control and orderliness in your financial life. Think of it like cleaning and organizing your room—when you know where everything is, you're able to feel more relaxed and don't wonder where you put your sunglasses.

If you think you're the only one who struggles to budget, you'd be wrong. People of all ages and income brackets find it hard. In fact, studies show that more than half of six-figure earners live paycheck to paycheck. In this chapter, I'll walk you through how to level up your budgeting game. You'll be a pro in no time.

CREATING YOUR SAVINGS GOALS

Before you get down to the finer points of budgeting, let's take a moment to look at the bigger picture of *what* you want to save for. When you're young, the idea of saving for the future can feel like this massive, never-ending mountain. But here's the thing: Once you start setting clear goals, it becomes a lot less intimidating—and a lot more doable.

5 STEPS TO SAVINGS SUCCESS

Whether you're saving for a summer vacation, your first car, or buying a home down the line, having a plan makes it easier to turn those goals into reality. Follow these five steps to set yourself up for savings success.

Step 1: Reflect on What You Want

What do you want to save for? Take a moment to think about what you want both in the short term and in the long term. There's an activity after this section to write down some of your savings goals.

Short-term goals could be things like building an emergency fund (page 61), buying a new laptop, or saving up for a trip. Long-term goals are those bigger, future-focused things like saving for a home down payment, or a car, or even planning for early retirement. (Yes, it's never too early to start thinking about that!)

Ask yourself: What do I want to accomplish in the next six months? What about in five years? Maybe you're dreaming of a trip to Mexico (honestly, same), or you want to start putting money away for that first big place of your own.

Step 2: Prioritize Your Goals

Now that you've got a list of savings goals, it's time to prioritize them. Some goals are more urgent than others, and that's okay. Focus on the ones that give you the most peace of mind, like setting up an emergency fund to cover unexpected expenses. But after that, it's vital to mix in the fun stuff, too. Use your gut feeling to rank your goals from highest priority to lowest.

Start with what's essential, but don't feel bad about also saving for something you're excited about. Maybe it's that dream vacation, a new gadget, or even setting aside money for self-care.

Step 3: Be Specific

Once you know what you're saving for and in what order, it's time to get specific. Write down the total amount you want to save, when you want to reach this goal, and how much you'll need to save per month to get there. (Hint: Divide the total amount by the number of months until your target date.) The more specific you can be, the easier it will be to track your progress.

Let's say it's September and you want to save $2,000 for a new laptop by next summer. That's about ten months away, so you'd need to save $200 a month to hit your goal.

Be specific with both the amount and the deadline. When you know exactly what you're working toward and when you want to get there, it'll feel more real and way more achievable.

Step 4: Split Big Goals into Smaller Steps

Some goals, like saving for a down payment on a house or building up a large emergency fund, might feel overwhelming. The key is to break down a big goal into smaller mini milestones.

For example, if your goal is to save $50,000 for a down payment, let's say you focus on saving the first $5,000 by the end of this year. The next year, you can aim to save another chunk.

Big goals don't have to be scary. By splitting them into smaller, more manageable steps, you can keep moving forward without feeling overwhelmed.

Step 5: Make a Plan and Track It

Once you've identified your goals, prioritized them, and created milestones, it's time to plan and track your progress. I'd recommend using a tool that works best for you, like an app or a spreadsheet to keep a running log of your savings goals and contributions. A notebook works well here. Set reminders on your phone to check in each month and make adjustments as needed. Don't forget to celebrate your wins—even if the progress is small, acknowledging it will help keep you motivated.

AUTOMATE YOUR SAVINGS

It can be so tempting to mindlessly swipe your bank card when your money's sitting in a checking account. However, it's harder to spend when your money is tucked away in your HYSA and not as easily accessible. The solution is to **automate** your savings.

It's fairly easy to set up a recurring transfer from your checking account to your HYSA. This is the process: Once your paycheck hits your checking account, your recurring transfer is sent from your checking to your HYSA. You control when you want this transfer to occur—every week, once a month—it's up to you. It's like "setting and forgetting" so that you don't have to think about transferring your savings, and it helps with maintaining your self-control. Ask your employer if your direct deposit paycheck can be routed into different bank accounts—some into checking and some into your HYSA.

You can also do the same thing for your bills and credit card statements. Some bill providers will even give you a small discount when you turn on autopay. I do this with my phone bill, and it works well. However, I'd only recommend automating your bill payments if you are sure of your finances each month and know that you have the money available in your account, so you don't incur overdraft fees.

Automating your financial life = one less thing on your plate!

Gen Z Reality Check

Figuring out your savings goals is one thing, but setting and actually sticking to a budget can be much trickier. In the pages ahead, you'll learn plenty of practical skills to help you out, but first, here's a vibe check from my community on the challenges of budgeting.

> "With everything digital, it's so easy to make quick, impulsive purchases or sign up for subscriptions and forget to cancel... It's a subtle drain on finances that's easy to underestimate."
>
> **—Annie, 24 years old**

> "Many of us are dealing with the pressure to build wealth quickly, partly driven by social media's portrayal of financial success and luxury lifestyles... Staying disciplined with budgeting and avoiding overspending on experiences or new trends can be difficult, even though I know these habits are crucial for building wealth."
>
> **—Austin, 22 years old**

> "I find [that] me and my friends tend to spend more than we want to, or even think about, due to not really having a place to look at what we are spending vs. what's coming in."
>
> **—Riley, 23 years old**

HOW TO LEVEL UP YOUR BUDGET

Budgeting is more than just managing your money—it's a way to bring peace and order to your financial life. Think of it as a form of self-care, similar to meal prepping for a busy week or setting aside time for mindfulness. A budget allows you to make intentional choices with your money, prioritizing what truly matters to you while easing financial stress. Instead of focusing on "cutting back," view your budget as a way to direct your spending toward what brings you joy and aligns with your values.

ONE MONTH TO BETTER BUDGETING

In the rush of life, it's easy to find yourself at the end of a pay cycle wondering "Wait, where did all my money go?"

I want to throw down a challenge that may sound like a lot at first: Track every dollar you earn and spend for a whole month. I promise it will be a game changer for your finances. It's going to take some discipline to complete this task, but by the end of the month you'll have a crystal-clear picture of your expenses and identify any sneaky money drains. This one-month experiment will give all information you need to create a new budget you can actually stick to.

Step 1: Track Every Dollar for a Month

When tracking your spending for the next month, don't overthink it. Go through your daily life and spend money where you normally do. Using a debit or credit card, it's pretty easy to see a summary of what you spent when you review your statements. Using physical cash? Be sure to log your purchases in a portable notebook or in the notes app on your phone so that you have a record.

Set a calendar reminder on your phone on Sunday night (or whichever day you prefer) to start a new spreadsheet (you can do this for free on Google Sheets) on your computer. Open your credit and/or debit card transactions for that week, or open your notebook where you've documented your purchases, and type in every buy you made that week, including the cost. Make sure to write down next to each purchase what the category was, such as rent, groceries, dining out, entertainment, shopping, debt payments, etc.

Simultaneously, keep a log of your after-tax income for the month: the dates, amount of income from all income sources, and where the income came from. Understanding how your money flows into your ecosystem is equally important in this exercise.

Step 2: Categorize and Reflect

It's time to review your totals after a month of expense tracking. In other words, how much did you spend in each category? Please don't judge yourself or the numbers you see (I know it's tempting to do so). Your goal here is to gather information about where you spend money so you can prioritize what's important to you and start making more intentional choices.

Once you figured out how much you spent in total and for your respective categories, I want you to (honestly) answer these questions:

Was my spending this month more or less than my income this month?

Which categories brought me the most joy this month? And the least?

Your spending should be less than your income. This is called "living within your means." With inflation and essentials like rent and food outpacing the growth of wages, it's completely understandable if there's not much leftover or none at all—that's okay, no shame here! But a good goal to set for yourself is for your income to outpace your spending.

There are no right or wrong answers to the second question—after all, the point of spending money is to enjoy your life. But I want you to think about the areas of your spending that are intentional and give you joy, as well as the areas where maybe you swiped your card that weren't so memorable. (*What was this purchase again?*) That's the whole point: Prioritize spending on the things that bring you joy and happiness, and deprioritize spending on things that don't give you much value. It's not about pinching pennies here.

Now that you have a clearer picture of where your money is going, it's time to get proactive—by building your new budget.

CREATING YOUR NEW BUDGET

Now that you've figured out your spending patterns, it's time to create your budget. When it comes to spending, you will have **fixed** expenses and **variable** expenses. Fixed expenses are those that reoccur monthly, meaning they don't change month to month. This typically includes your rent or mortgage, utilities, car payments, groceries, etc. Variable expenses could change month to month, like eating out, shopping, entertainment, and the like. Fixed expenses are hard to change, but variable expenses are easier to control.

In terms of reducing costs, there are several ways you can go about it. For fixed expenses, you can consider any opportunities to negotiate or reduce. For instance, you might be able to bundle your internet and phone services for a discount or cancel subscriptions you don't use. For variable expenses, identify small swaps that add up over time—like cooking more at home rather than relying on food delivery apps or switching to generic brands for certain items. Remember, this doesn't mean that you can't enjoy a latte at your local cafe or never treat yourself to a brand you love.

This is about identifying and reining in those frequent expenses that make it harder for you to balance your budget.

There are two main methods for budgeting to consider:

The 50/30/20 budget: This is a budgeting method where you allocate 50% for needs, 30% for wants, and 20% for savings or debt. However, this is a general formula for you to follow. It's not a one-size-fits-all approach. You can always adjust the percentages to fit your situation.

Zero-based budgeting: This budgeting method involves giving every dollar a "job," where you're allocating every dollar of your income to a category (including savings), until you reach zero. A simple example: Say you make $3,000 a month. You might put $1,000 in rent, $300 into groceries, $300 into savings, and so on. By the end your income minus expenses equals zero.

When building your budget, don't forget to consider what is and isn't important to you. Here are some helpful things to consider.

- **Top three spending priorities:** What categories are non-negotiable for you? This could be anything from savings to travel or fitness. Rank them to make sure your budget aligns with your values.

- **Fun fund:** Consider setting aside a small, fixed amount each month for "fun" spending. This is guilt-free money for hobbies, treats, or spontaneous outings that bring joy.

- **Smarter spending:** Make cuts in areas that don't serve you well. If you rarely remember a purchase, it might not be worth repeating. The goal is to create a budget that reflects *you*.

If you have debt payments, it's also important to prioritize those in your monthly budget to ensure you're keeping up with at least the minimum payments. (More details about debt and loans in Chapters 5 and 6.)

In Chapter 3, we explored setting up your savings and creating your emergency fund. Creating a budget is the perfect time to incorporate how much you're putting away toward those goals. Create separate savings buckets and line items for these goals in your budget to keep track of the portions of income that go toward each of them. If you are putting money toward investments, you can include that in your budget, too. (More about investments in Chapter 7.)

Here's an example of how a budget could look for someone in their mid-twenties who is new to budgeting:

CATEGORY	BUDGETED	ACTUAL
FIXED EXPENSES		
Rent/Mortgage	$1,200	$1,200
Utilities	$150	$140
Groceries	$300	$280
Internet/Phone	$100	$100
Car Payment	$200	$200
VARIABLE EXPENSES		
Dining Out	$200	$250
Entertainment	$100	$120
Shopping	$150	$130
DEBT PAYMENTS		
Credit Card Payment	$100	$100
Student Loan Payment	$200	$200
SAVINGS/INVESTMENTS		
Emergency Fund	$150	$150
Retirement Fund	$200	$200
Travel Fund	$100	$100
TOTAL	**$3,150**	**$3,170**

ADJUST YOUR BUDGET AS NEEDED

Budgets are not fixed. When your income or rent changes or you have different spending priorities, it's okay to change your budget. If you're changing and growing, so should your budget. Check into your budget each month and tweak the category amounts as needed to best align them with your goals.

Also, don't forget to acknowledge and celebrate your wins, no matter how small. "Treat yo' self" with something small but meaningful when you hit a savings goal.

Tools for Budgeting Success

Using the right tools can make a big difference. Here are some ideas of apps and tools to help manage your budget:

- **Apps and websites:** There are several companies and developers who specialize in creating budgeting software and tools that automatically sync your bank and credit card information to create your budget. A few popular options include Copilot, Monarch Money, and You Need a Budget (YNAB).

- **Spreadsheet templates:** If you prefer a DIY method, creating your own spreadsheet can be a rewarding way to manually track income and expenses. You can start with a simple Google Sheet and customize as you get more familiar with your habits.

- **The envelope system (aka "cash stuffing"):** This budgeting technique involves taking physical cash and dividing it among envelopes for each of your budget categories. It helps you avoid spending beyond what you planned and is a good system for impulse spenders who struggle to stick to a budget.

PUT IT INTO ACTION:
ROAD TEST YOUR NEW BUDGET

Now that you're clearer on budgeting, it's time to road test your new budget. Following, you'll find a blank budgeting table that you can use to get started. Take a moment to fill in the table with your own numbers.

Here's what to do:

1. **Fill in your income.** In the first row, write down all your sources of income for the month. This could include your salary, freelance work, side hustles, or any other income streams.

2. **List your fixed expenses.** These are the non-negotiable costs you pay every month—think rent, utilities, insurance, and groceries.

3. **List your variable expenses.** These costs can change month to month, such as dining out, entertainment, shopping, or hobbies.

4. **Add savings and debt payments.** Include any money you're putting toward savings goals, emergency funds, or paying down debt.

5. **Review your total.** Tally up each column to see how your planned budget compares to your actual spending. How do these numbers align with your financial goals? Are there categories of spending that surprise you or stand out as areas to adjust? Use this as a starting point to fine-tune your budget, ensuring it reflects your priorities.

Here's a blank table to get you started.

CATEGORY	MONTHLY BUDGET	ACTUAL SPENDING
INCOME		
Salary/Primary Income		
Side Hustles/Freelance		
Other:		
FIXED EXPENSES		
Rent/Mortgage		
Utilities		
Groceries		
Internet/Phone		
Insurance (Car/Health)		
Subscriptions		
Other:		
VARIABLE EXPENSES		
Dining Out		
Entertainment		
Shopping		
Personal Care/Hobbies		
Other:		
DEBT PAYMENTS		
Credit Card Payment		
Student Loan Payment		
Other:		
SAVINGS/INVESTMENTS		
Emergency Fund		
Retirement Fund		
Travel/Big Purchases		
Other:		

Isaiah Learns to "Pay Yourself First"

Meet Isaiah, a 24-year-old software developer who always seemed to be living paycheck to paycheck. Despite earning a solid income, he often scrambled to cover bills by the end of the month. Most of his money went toward spontaneous weekend trips, dining out with friends, and upgrading the latest gadgets. The thing is, he didn't track his spending and pretty much swiped his credit card whenever he saw fit. When he did check his bank account, his credit card debt and his lack of savings bothered him, but he didn't change his spending habits.

The wake-up call came when his car broke down, leaving him with a $1,500 repair bill he couldn't afford. Isaiah was forced to ask his family to help him foot the bill. Feeling embarrassed and frustrated, Isaiah vowed to never end up in this situation again.

He began with the fundamentals, carefully tracking his expenses for a month. He was surprised at what he saw. While reviewing his spending, he was overspending on entertainment and impulse buys without even realizing it.

He started a budget on an online spreadsheet to first prioritize his essentials. He made sure to include a savings category where he would "pay himself first" into a high-yield savings account before spending money on his "wants" categories. He also set aside a separate "fun fund" for guilt-free spending on hobbies he loved, like gaming.

Six months later, Isaiah had saved up for a modest emergency fund, paid off his credit card debt, and managed to automate his savings for the first time. He felt a newfound sense of security and pride, recognizing that budgeting wasn't about denying himself—it was about gaining control and preparing for the unexpected.

WAYS TO SAVE FOR YOUR BUDGET

Of course, saving money doesn't have to mean giving up everything you enjoy. It's more about making small changes in areas where the spending doesn't really serve you. A few tweaks here and there can add up fast and help you reach your goals sooner. Here's a quick list of questions to ask yourself before making a purchase, plus some common areas where people tend to overspend and ways to save on them.

Questions to ask yourself before you buy something:

Do I really need this, or is it just a nice-to-have?

Will I still be happy with this purchase a month from now?

Could I find it for less, or do I already own something similar?

Does this align with my financial goals right now?

These questions aren't about talking yourself out of everything, but it's about spending with intention. If it still feels worth it, go for it!

Everyday expenses where you can save:

Car insurance: Shopping around every 6 to 12 months can lead to better deals. Bundling home or renter's insurance with the same provider often saves money, too, so it's worth a look.

Subscriptions: You know those subscriptions that just keep renewing? It's a good habit to check in every few months to see if you're actually using them. If not, go ahead and cancel. Check your bank account or your phone subscriptions.

Cell phone plan: If you're not using all the data or features on your plan, it might be time to switch to something smaller (or a budget-friendly provider). Smaller carriers offer competitive plans that are usually way cheaper.

Utilities: Little things like using LED bulbs or unplugging devices or small appliances when not in use can lower your monthly bill.

Some utility providers even offer discounts or rebates on energy-saving items.

Groceries: Plan meals and make a list before you shop. It helps avoid random purchases, and you'd be surprised how much you can save over time. Buying in bulk can also be a win, especially for pantry staples (that's what Costco's for).

Credit card interest: If you have a balance, look into options with lower rates, like a balance transfer. Paying it down as fast as possible saves you from paying all that extra interest. (More on this on page 106.)

KEEPING UP WITH THE JENNERS

The phrase, "keeping up with the Joneses" is about comparing what you have to your neighbors or people in your immediate circle. Now thanks to social media, we have access to details of everyone's lives, including celebrities. We have access to their every day, what they were, where they are going. With that kind of unfettered access, it's easy to fall into the temptation of comparing yourself to anyone and everyone.

Look no further than the Kardashian and Jenner families, whose reality TV show *Keeping Up with the Kardashians* shows off their lavish lifestyles. I remember seeing various tabloid photos of them sporting Himalayan Birkin bags (I think it's made of crocodile skin or something?), which costs *just* the small amount of $400,000. This is a super tiny amount of their overall net worth, but most of us don't have Kardashian or Jenner money, unfortunately.

We're constantly exposed to curated snapshots of people's highlight reels, which can create a sense of envy. It's natural to feel like everyone else has it all figured out, but remember, everyone's just putting out their best show. Social media is not real life. You don't know what someone is actually going through behind the camera. Influencers and even friends often only share the best parts of their lives. When you catch yourself in the comparison trap, try to pause and ask: *Do I want this because it fits my goals or because it seems like everyone else has it?*

As a chronically online person, I have to be intentionally mindful of my consumption of other people's content for this very reason. But a great thing about social media is that you can follow people whose content resonates with you the most. You can curate your feed to what makes you feel good and unfollow those whose content doesn't add value to your life. The rules are yours!

Comparison can lead us to spend on things just to feel like we're "keeping up." Online shopping and "buy now, pay later" services (page 85) have made it easier than ever to make quick impulse purchases, with items arriving at our doors within days. Next time when you see something you want to buy online, ask yourself, "Does this purchase add value to my life?" Keep the item in your virtual cart for several days and come back to it. Do you still care about it, or was it an impulsive thought at the moment?

Try setting specific savings goals or spending priorities and remind yourself of them when you're tempted by the latest trend. I'd suggest you write your goals somewhere visible (like on the notes app in your phone) so you have easy access to remind yourself of those goals! By staying true to your own path, you'll avoid the regret that often follows envy-driven purchases. Remember: True success isn't about keeping up with others—it's about creating a life that feels right for you.

SAVE MORE WITH LOUD BUDGETING

Essentially, loud budgeting means that you vocalize to your friends and family (or even publicly for #accountability) what fits in your budget and what doesn't.

Say your friends decide to buy last-minute tickets to a music festival that costs $140, but you are nearly out of spending money until payday. Instead of deciding to go anyway or making up a polite excuse, you would instead tell them that you won't be joining because you don't have the budget. It may feel awkward at first, but this practice empowers you to set financial boundaries and spend intentionally, focusing on the areas that genuinely bring you joy instead of things you feel pressured to do.

Here are a couple of ways you can embrace loud budgeting into your own life:

- **Set spending priorities and stick to them.** Make it known what you prioritize in your budget. For example, if travel is important to you, share that with friends and family. When they know your spending priorities, they're more likely to understand if you opt out of other activities.

- **Celebrate financial wins together.** Loud budgeting doesn't have to be about restrictions—it's also a chance to share wins with those you trust. Whether it's hitting a savings milestone or paying off a credit card, celebrating openly with your circle reinforces positive financial habits and keeps you motivated.

BUY NOW, PAY LATER

If you've shopped online, chances are you've seen the option of "pay for this item in four installments" during the checkout process. Some of the popular companies that offer this service include Affirm, Afterpay, and Klarna, and they fall under the term "**buy now, pay later**" or **BNPL** for short. Essentially, BNPL allows you to buy something right away but pay for it over time in installments (it's basically a short-term consumer loan). BNPL has become extremely popular within the last few years, especially through social media platforms like TikTok and as more people turn to online shopping.

BNPL usage has skyrocketed. According to the Federal Reserve, 14% of Americans used BNPL in 2023, up from 12% in

2022. Gen Z is the age group most likely to use it. The appeal lies in the convenience of 0% interest on loans, no credit checks, and instant gratification. It makes shopping feel easy because it seems like you're paying less upfront while getting the item right away.

However, using BNPL can turn into slippery slope *very* quickly. It can lead you to buying things you can't afford and land you in consumer debt. The way BNPL is marketed is quite predatory, encouraging people to spend what they don't have. You know things are getting out of hand when Chipotle offers BNPL for a $15 burrito! Plus, if you miss a repayment, you can be stung with big late fees. Additionally, paying off a BNPL loan won't help you establish credit, and it doesn't offer the protections of a credit card (more on that later in the next chapter).

Here's a summary of the pros and cons of BNPL:

PROS OF BNPL	CONS OF BNPL
✓ 0% interest on certain plans	✗ Can lead to over-spending or debt
✓ No credit checks	✗ Won't help establish credit
✓ Convenient for big purchases (if you can realistically pay it off)	✗ Lacks credit card protections

I'm not saying you should completely avoid BNPL. For some, it's a helpful tool for managing big purchases responsibly. But for most people, using BNPL isn't necessary and often leads to more harm than good. Use it in moderation, and only if you're confident you can pay off the installments.

5 Signs You Are Better with Money Than You Think

When we constantly compare ourselves to what others have or what they are doing, we often forget to appreciate and celebrate our own financial wins. Here are five signs you're actually better with money than you think:

1. **You have $1,000 (or more) in savings.** Almost 50% of Americans can't afford a $1,000 emergency expense. If you have a thousand dollars or more saved, you're doing better than most. If you don't, this is a good first goal to set on your savings journey.

2. **You've built an emergency fund.** This shows you've achieved a high level of financial discipline and means you don't have to stress about immediate or unexpected expenses (see page 61).

3. **You have money left over after paying bills.** This means you're in a good spot because you have disposable income left over to spend, save, or invest.

4. **You avoid high-interest debt.** By paying off credit card balances in full each month, you avoid costly interest, keep debt in check, and have greater financial flexibility.

5. **You understand your credit report and score.** Your credit score influences a lot of the things you can do, like getting a car, renting an apartment, getting a mortgage, and sometimes even getting a job! Knowing your score—and how to improve it—empowers you to make informed financial choices (see page 113).

STAYING ON TRACK WITH YOUR BUDGET

When you first create a budget, it's exciting and motivating. Your goals and your why for creating a budget are still fresh in your mind. But like any new habit, the initial thrill can wear off, making it challenging to stick to your budget over a longer period of time, especially when unexpected expenses pop up or motivation dips.

COMMON BUDGET PITFALLS

Here are some common pitfalls people face with budgeting—and strategies to help you stay on track:

Pitfall #1: Losing Motivation

One of the biggest hurdles with budgeting is that the excitement often fades after the first few months. At first, it's motivating to see progress, but as time goes on, it can start to feel routine or restrictive.

Strategy: Set small, achievable goals along the way to keep up your motivation. Break down larger goals into monthly or even weekly milestones and celebrate each win—no matter how small. For example, if you're working on building an emergency fund, give yourself a small treat when you reach each $500 saved.

Pitfall #2: Unexpected Expenses

Life has a way of surprising us with unexpected costs, from car repairs to last-minute travel needs. These expenses can throw a carefully planned budget into a loop.

Strategy: Build a buffer into your budget for unplanned expenses. Set aside a small amount each month specifically for unexpected costs. Even a modest buffer of $50 or $100 a month can help you stay on track without dipping into savings or relying on credit when surprises pop up.

Pitfall #3: Feeling Restricted and Having "Budget Burnout"

Budgeting can sometimes feel like a constant series of limitations, which can lead to feelings of restriction and eventually "budget burnout." This burnout can make it tempting to abandon your budget entirely.

Strategy: Regularly revisit your "why." Take a few minutes each month to remind yourself of the bigger reasons behind your budget, whether that's building financial security, saving for a big goal, or reducing money stress. You can try techniques like creating a vision board or writing down your top financial goals (on a notebook or sticky notes) and keep it somewhere visible. This reminder can help re-center you, keeping you focused on what budgeting allows you to achieve rather than what it limits.

TAKEAWAYS

THE NEW RULES OF BUDGETING

Saving money doesn't have to mean saying no to the small things in life that bring you joy. Instead of viewing budgeting as a form of restriction, see it through a lens of empowerment: It puts you in charge of your savings goals.

OLD RULES	NEW RULES
Spend what you need, then save what you can	Automate your savings so funds stay out of temptation's reach
The more you restrict your spending, the more you save	The more realistic your budget, the more likely you are to stick with it
Friends and family should always come before my finances	It's okay to set healthy financial boundaries with friends and family
Social media shows you what you should aspire to in life	Avoid comparing your life to the curated lives of others on social media to reduce FOMO spending
"Buy now, pay later" is a safe way to spend	"Buy now, pay later" increases your likelihood of overspending and ending up in debt

(5)

CREDIT AND DEBT? DON'T SWEAT

redit card bills. Student loans. Life curveballs. The truth is, debt is a reality for many of us today. Even with the best planning, people sometimes find themselves in debt from situations out of their control, such as medical bills. In other cases, many people didn't learn about spending habits and debt because these topics are often not taught to us properly at home or school.

Not all debt is created equal. There's the type that can open doors, and then there's the type that can drain your bank account faster than you can say "minimum payment due." But debt, when used wisely, can be a tool for building your future—whether earning a degree, buying a home, or launching a business.

This chapter will cover everything—from the basics of "good" vs. "bad" debt to proven strategies for paying down what you owe. And we'll explore how to use credit to your advantage without getting trapped in the cycle of high-interest payments. You're not alone if you've ever felt overwhelmed or unsure about your debt. But with knowledge and a solid plan, you can flip debt from a setback into a stepping stone.

NOT ALL DEBT IS CREATED EQUAL

When someone says "debt," it usually comes with a negative connotation, but that's not the case with all types of debt. Avoiding debt altogether is unrealistic for everyone because sometimes that is the only option, especially for more significant purchases such as houses or cars. In 2024, Gen Zers carried an average debt of around $16,000, so having and dealing with debt is more common than you think.

"GOOD" DEBT

"Good" debt usually involves a low interest rate and typically helps finance a purchase that can generate future income or return. Low-interest loans include mortgages, student loans, and business loans. Essentially, these types of loans are framed as investments in the future. However, you should decide how much "good" debt you can reasonably take on and create a plan to repay it.

A home loan: Buying a house is the financial pinnacle of the American Dream. Unfortunately, the price of buying a home has significantly outpaced wage growth. Many people don't consider buying a home until later in life, which makes sense. The value of a home usually grows over several decades, which outpaces the cost of the home loan (mortgage). A mortgage comes with an interest rate, which determines the extra amount you pay on top of the cost of the loan. Interest rates fluctuate greatly depending on the health of the housing market and the greater economy. They can range from as low as 2% to as high as 8%. We'll explore home loans more in the next chapter.

Student loans: This is one of the most common forms of "good" debt for young people, and the primary way to pay for higher education. You take out a student loan, hoping that your future job or career earnings will earn a return on investment (ROI). That investment is what you spend to get your education or degree. We'll also look at student loans in more detail in the next chapter.

"BAD" DEBT

"Bad" debt is a loan that typically has high interest rates, doesn't generate future returns or income, and can be difficult to repay on time, making it a financial burden rather than an investment. These include high-interest credit card debt, car payments, and other consumer debt, which can keep people in a cycle of debt that can be hard to break out of. Remember that it doesn't mean *you* are bad if you have bad debt. It's a temporary obstacle you can overcome, not a moral failing.

Credit card debt: This can be one of the costliest due to high interest rates, usually 20% or more. If you're carrying a balance on your credit card and unable to pay it off, it has the potential to snowball into debt that quickly balloons to become significant and costly.

Payday loans: These are high-interest, short-term loans under $500 and are typically due on the borrower's next payday. People usually get this type of loan if they don't have enough money to pay for expenses between paydays. However, these types of loans are predatory. Lenders often charge $10 to $30 for every $100 you borrow for two weeks. Paying this charge across an entire year is like having a credit card with an APR (annual percentage rate) of 390%. Bonkers! Unfortunately, payday loan vendors often target low-income communities.

High-interest car loans: Car loans aren't inherently "bad." This line item in a person's budget is manageable, especially if you need a car. They can range from 4% to 20%, depending on the strength of your credit score. We'll go into more detail about credit scores in this chapter. However, a car is considered a "depreciating asset," meaning it loses value when you drive it off the dealer's lot. If you have a car loan for an extended period of time, it's completely possible your outstanding auto loan balance can become more than what the car is worth, which can happen to both new and used car loans. The best approach is to understand what car fits into your budget and lifestyle and what you can reasonably afford on your income to manage the monthly payment.

Gen Z Reality Check

You're not alone if you feel like you're just figuring out credit and debt as you go. Many Gen Zers didn't get the financial education they deserved growing up, making it harder to manage debt and save. I asked my community for their thoughts, and here's what they said.

"Some people are lucky they had that foundation in their households growing up, but others (like me) have struggled to manage a credit card because we don't understand the foundation/the basics of how and why the system works."

—María José, 21 years old

"When I first got a part-time job, my immigrant parents didn't know much about finance except that I should set aside money to save. Even now as a Gen Zer with a full-time job, I still struggle to save and pay off debt because I don't have that knowledge or didn't have that education surrounding finance."

—Allysha, 26 years old

"I sometimes fall into a 'YOLO' mindset, justifying frequent indulgences like sweet treats or online shopping as well-deserved rewards. Although I manage to pay off my credit card debt on time, saving is difficult because I often dip into my savings to cover my wants rather than my needs."

—Maria Sofia, 19 years old

THE GAME PLAN TO TACKLE DEBT

It can be a lot to balance paying off debt while saving for the future and simultaneously satisfying your current needs. If you're finding it difficult to maintain this equation, consider life if you were debt-free: "What could I do with an extra $X per month? What would my dream life look like?" Understanding your "why" for paying off debt (your purpose, goals, etc.) can motivate you when times get tough. This section is about shifting how you view debt, setting a strategy, and giving concrete steps to tackle it head-on. Let's do this together!

MAPPING OUT YOUR PLAN

Here are the first steps to help you organize and tackle your debt:

Make a debt list. List all your debts, including the creditor, balance, interest rate (APR), and minimum monthly payment. Adding up the totals can be scary, but I urge you to complete this task. Seeing your debt laid out in front of you is a vital starting point for regaining control. Keeping this information in a spreadsheet or notebook that tracks your debt helps you stay organized.

Understand your monthly cash flow. Examine your income and expenses to determine how much money you have after covering essential costs. This will help you decide what to allocate to debt repayment. Start by identifying how much of your income is available after paying for necessities like rent, groceries, utilities, and transportation. This will give you a clear picture of your financial room to maneuver.

Check your budget. After understanding your cash flow, you can adjust your budget. Are there categories where you can reallocate money, like reducing your discretionary expenses? You can also consider finding ways to increase your income if you want to prioritize paying off debt more quickly. This is where you set aside the amount you can consistently dedicate to paying down debt and adjust your budget to align with your debt payoff goals. For a reminder on how to set up your budget, revisit Chapter 4.

Pick a strategy. The avalanche and snowball repayment methods are popular. The following pages will provide more options.

Here's an example of what your debt list might look like:

DEBT	BALANCE	INTEREST RATE	MINIMUM MONTHLY PAYMENT
Car loan	$8,000	5%	$250
Student loan	$20,000	6%	$220
Credit card	$2,000	20%	$150
Total	**$30,000**		**$620**

THE AVALANCHE METHOD: TARGETING HIGH-INTEREST DEBT FIRST

The **avalanche method** is a strategy for paying off the debt that costs you the most in interest payments. First, pay off the debt with the highest interest rate while making minimum payments on your other obligations. This reduces the overall interest you'll pay, speeding up your path to becoming debt-free. Here's how to use the avalanche method:

1. **List your debts.** Write down all your debts, including balances, interest rates (APRs), and minimum monthly payments.

2. **Order by interest rate.** Arrange your debts from the highest interest rate to the lowest.

3. **Make minimum payments.** Pay the minimum required on all debts to avoid penalties or late fees.

4. Attack the highest-interest debt. Put any extra money you have toward the debt with the highest interest rate. Once that's paid off, move to the next highest.

Here's an example: Let's say you have three debts:

- Credit Card A with a $4,000 balance at 20% APR

- Credit Card B with a $3,000 balance at 15% APR

- A personal loan of $7,000 at 8% APR

With the avalanche method, you'd first focus on paying off Credit Card A. After it's paid off, you'd shift your attention to Credit Card B and, finally, the personal loan.

There are both upsides and downsides to the avalanche method. Since it saves you the most money on interest, it's the most cost-effective strategy in the long term. However, if your highest-interest debt also has a large balance, it can initially feel like there's slow progress. The hardest part is staying motivated, but tracking your interest savings over time can provide powerful motivation and remind you that your hard work and discipline are making a significant impact. This could help free up your budget to save and invest more toward your goals.

THE SNOWBALL METHOD: BUILD MOMENTUM WITH QUICK WINS

If seeing fast results motivates you, the **snowball method** could be your perfect match. This strategy is about first paying off the smallest debts to build up your momentum and confidence.

Here's how you can use the snowball method:

1. **List your debts.** Write down all your debts, including balances, interest rates (APRs), and minimum monthly payments.

2. **Order by balance.** Arrange your debts from the smallest to the largest.

3. **Make minimum payments.** Pay the minimum required on all debts to stay current.

4. **Tackle the smallest debt first.** Use any extra money to pay off the smallest debt. Then, move on to the next smallest debt and repeat.

Let's go back to the same example:

- Credit Card A with a $4,000 balance at 20% APR

- Credit Card B with a $3,000 balance at 15% APR

- A personal loan of $7,000 at 8% APR.

The snowball method first focuses on Credit Card B because it has the smallest balance. After paying it off, you'd move on to Credit Card A and the personal loan.

The main benefit of the snowball method is the psychological boost of quick wins. Paying off smaller debts quickly can give you a sense of accomplishment and the motivation to keep going. On the downside, this method may cost you more interest over time than the avalanche method. But for many people, the feeling of progress and seeing debts disappear is more than worth it.

Whatever method you choose, it's key to stay consistent and celebrate every milestone. Every debt paid off—big or small—is one step closer to financial freedom.

Ghosting Your Debt?
(You're Not Alone)

Hiding from your debt is a common response among people who have much of it. Maybe you ignore credit card statements after spending a lot of money or avoid thinking about your balance. This tendency to "ghost" debt is more common than you think, and there's even a name for it: the "Ostrich Effect." Like an ostrich burying its head in the sand, people sometimes pretend debt isn't there because it's too anxiety-inducing, and they hope it will somehow disappear. But I'm here to tell you that this type of magical thinking, avoiding your debt, will only result in more debt and more significant problems down the road.

Again, debt doesn't reflect your personal worth or a moral failing. The fact that you acknowledge your debt and want to change your situation is a significant first step!

It's also important to recognize that debt isn't just an individual problem—it's a systemic one. Lack of financial education leaves many people vulnerable. Predatory lending practices or high-interest credit products can trap people in cycles of debt. Know that this isn't your fault.

The good news? You don't have to face debt alone. You've taken the first step just by reading this book and looking to improve your financial situation, and that's something to be proud of.

BANK CARDS 101

When it comes to the topic of **credit cards**, there is a big problem of spending and credit card dependence in America. When misused, credit cards can cause an extreme cycle of debt that could be particularly hard to climb out of. Forty-nine percent of American households carry credit card debt, with an average balance of $6,501. *But*, if you understand how credit cards work and use them responsibly, they can be a valuable financial tool.

When you open an account with a bank like Chase, Wells Fargo, or Citi, you're typically issued a **debit card** with your account. When you swipe your debit card at the register, money is taken directly from your checking account to pay for your purchase.

PROS AND CONS OF DEBIT CARDS

PROS	CONS
✓ **Direct access to funds:** Debit cards allow you to spend money straight from your checking account. ✓ **Lower fees:** There are fewer chances of incurring interest charges due to low fees of debit cards. ✓ **No credit check:** Getting a debit card usually doesn't require a credit check, making it accessible for those with poor or no credit history. ✓ **No risk of debt:** Using a debit card prevents overspending and accumulating debt since you are limited to your available balance.	✗ **Limited fraud protection:** There is limited fraud protection on debit cards compared to credit cards in cases of theft and damages to goods. ✗ **Overdraft fees:** Spending more than what's available in your account balance using a debit can trigger fees (you can opt-out of overdraft coverage). ✗ **Less credit history:** Using a debit card doesn't build your credit history. ✗ **Less reward potential:** Debit cards generally offer fewer rewards or cash back compared to credit cards.

You can think of using a credit card as a short-term loan. A debit card uses money from your bank account to make purchases. A credit card is like borrowing money from the company that gave you the card. You are responsible for paying off your balance in full before the statement due date (typically every 30 days). Interest charges will apply if you carry a balance past the due date.

PROS AND CONS OF CREDIT CARDS

PROS	CONS
✓ **Build credit history:** You can build credit and increase your credit score by using a credit card responsibly.	✗ **Debt risk:** There's a risk of going into debt with credit cards if you overspend and don't pay off the balance in full every month.
✓ **Rewards and benefits:** Many credit cards offer rewards programs, cash back, travel points, and other perks for spending.	✗ **High-interest rates:** Credit cards have some of the highest interest rates and using them can lead to significant amounts of debt by carrying a balance.
✓ **Travel benefits:** Some credit cards come with travel benefits like access to airport lounges and travel credits, and no foreign transaction fees.	✗ **Fees:** The fees can add up—many credit cards charge annual fees, late payment fees, and foreign transaction fees.
✓ **Purchase protection:** Many credit cards offer purchase protections, which can allow you to replace or refund an item that's been stolen or damaged.	✗ **Credit score impact:** Your credit score can be negatively impacted if you miss payments or accumulate high balances.

Beware of Online Scams

I recently visited Paris, but I didn't plan any sightseeing excursions until a few days before the trip (I'm more of a "we'll do as we feel" kind of traveler). Close to the trip's date, I tried to get tickets to the Louvre, the famous museum with the original Mona Lisa in it.

But it was down when I went to the official website to purchase the tickets. Frantically (because I had no time left), I went to a third-party site to get the tickets. Turns out, they were scam tickets. We were denied entry into the museum and lost hundreds of dollars.

My credit card company refunded me because I used a credit card with purchase protection. Still, I learned an important lesson about being careful with third-party websites.

Always shop on secure websites to protect yourself from online credit card fraud. Look for "https" in the URL and a padlock symbol. Also, review your credit card statements regularly for unauthorized transactions. Contact your credit card company if you spot any unfamiliar charges.

CHOOSING A CREDIT CARD

I began my credit-building journey when I was 18 and entering college. I started with a **secured credit card**, which can often be found at most major banks, credit unions, or credit card companies. This type of card requires you to put some skin in the game in the form of an initial deposit. This helps you unlock a line of credit to start using. The amount you're required to put down is typically the amount of credit you get. For example, your secured credit card lets you put $250 down. This means you'll get $250 in credit to use. The amount of credit you get can vary depending on the issuer, but it can range from several hundred to a few thousand dollars. You can put small purchases and bills on the card and make sure you pay off the card on time.

This method is excellent for helping you build credit in a reasonable and contained way. Paying off your monthly debt shows the credit card company that you're a reliable borrower. Your credit score will increase, and eventually you can upgrade to a credit card with a higher credit limit and more rewards.

Tips on Using a Credit Card

When using a credit card, here are some things to keep in mind to use one responsibly. I follow these rules religiously:

Always pay off the statement balance and NOT just the minimum balance. On your credit card statement, you will see two numbers—a **statement balance** and a **minimum balance**. Many younger adults don't understand that if you pay only the minimum balance, you will start to accrue interest on the balance. Make sure you pay off the *statement* balance in full every month. I check my bank app every week (I know, I'm paranoid) to pay off my balance, or you could also set up your payments on autopay so that your statement gets paid off automatically for you.

Check your banking app weekly to review your transactions and look for fraud. As mentioned, this ensures you recognize your transactions. If you suspect any suspicious activity, contact your bank ASAP to freeze your card and find out about refund options.

Credit from a credit card is NOT free money. The money you spend on a credit card is a *loan*, under your name, *not money*. Only spend money on a credit card that you have the funds for. This is why building up an emergency fund is essential, so you don't need to rely on a credit card when money gets tight.

Understand your spending habits and tendencies. If you struggle with impulse spending, I strongly suggest using only *one* credit card. This can help trick your mind into thinking you have less money to spend. Regarding management, things are also a lot simpler with just one card. Cut up the cards you no longer use and delete saved cards on your account or Apple Pay. Less clutter means more peace of mind.

Rewards Cards

Have you ever seen videos of people discussing travel hacks and how they travel "for free"? They're typically talking about using **reward points** from credit cards to pay for their flights or hotels. The subsequent online applications ask for your income and credit score to be eligible for higher reward cards. Depending on your answers, they may accept or reject your application. Certain credit cards require higher credit scores and/or incomes.

There are various rewards card tiers, but most give you points every time you make a purchase. The points can be used to exchange for cash, statement credits, flight transfers to an airline portal, and more. The higher-end travel credit cards even provide access to nice lounges at the airport, hotel and flight credits, and shopping credits. The list continues—think of it like a premium coupon book. These cards charge an annual fee, but if you use all the benefits provided by the card, it can be well worth it.

Rewards cards provide perks, but there are also downsides. Since these cards are more "premium," they often come with higher credit (or borrowing) limits. If not used wisely, it can be really easy to rack up credit card debt. However, if you are a responsible credit card user, these types of cards may actually help you make a net positive.

MONTHLY CREDIT CARD PAYMENTS

By paying off your credit card balance in full each month, you clear the debt on the card and avoid paying interest. If you don't pay off the balance each month, you go into credit card debt and can become subject to something called "compound interest," which is when interest is earned on the principal *and* the accumulated interest of a loan. Compound interest benefits you when you invest your money (more on that in Chapter 7 on page 155), but it can be damaging when it comes to credit card debt because the interest rate is so high.

Let's look at how interest payments can play out when it comes to credit card debt, and why it's dangerous. Your balance on a credit card compounds through a daily interest rate. Let me explain. If the APR on your credit card is 20%, then your daily interest rate is 20% / 365 days = 0.0548%.

Let's use a monthly payment balance of $1,000. If you missed the due date, after one day with the APR applied, your updated balance is $1,000.06 (which includes 6 cents in interest). After 30 days, assuming your balance is untouched, you end up with a balance of $1,016.57.

The first day of interest is 6 cents. In linear progression, that would equate to $0.06 x 30 = $1.80 in interest. However, with the power of daily compounding, the interest snowballs to $16.57. ($14.77 more than a linear progression!) That's because the interest per day is calculated on the *previous day's total balance.*

HOW TO SPOT (LEGAL) CREDIT TRAPS

Credit cards can be helpful tools, but they can also come with traps that make it easy to slip into debt. While some predatory practices may be illegal, many sneaky tactics used by credit card companies are perfectly legal—and can leave you financially vulnerable if you're not careful.

One common trap is credit cards with **teaser rates**. These cards might offer a low introductory interest rate, sometimes even 0%, but once the promotion ends, the interest can skyrocket. Many people aren't prepared for this sudden change and end up paying much more in interest than expected. Make sure to read the fine print carefully, especially when it comes to introductory offers.

Credit card agreements can also come with **high fees** or **complex terms** that aren't always obvious. They are laced with terms around late payment fees, balance transfers, and cash advances. If not careful, ignoring these terms can push you (further) into debt.

Another potential pitfall is unexpected increases in your **credit limit**. While it may seem like a gift, higher limits can lead to higher spending. This could lead to spending beyond one's means and accumulating debt beyond your means of repayment.

Have you ever received a credit card in the mail (Macy's, Nordstrom, and the like) with advertising that says "get 20% off your first purchase if you sign up for our credit card"? Don't do it. **Store credit cards** are another example of enticing traps. They often come with immediate discounts at checkout, which is why they seem tempting. However, these types of cards frequently have high interest rates and low credit limits.

Finally, many credit card companies aggressively market their products to college students at fairs or through targeted promotions. They tend to target students because they are a more vulnerable group, and the companies know most students didn't learn about credit or personal finance in school.

Tip: Always read the terms and conditions, and be wary of offers that seem too good to be true. Taking a step back before accepting any credit offer can help protect you from falling into a debt trap.

BREAKING THE CREDIT CARD DEBT CYCLE

If you're currently in the credit card debt cycle, it can feel like a lot to handle at first. But here are ways to regain control of your finances and break free from the debt spiral.

First, you need to make getting out of debt a priority in your life. It's really easy to keep putting it off versus facing the situation head-on. Many people struggle to change their habits because it feels challenging, and it feels easier to just fall back into old habits. But by committing and recommitting to learning and genuinely setting a goal for yourself, you're already making great progress.

Next, assess your situation honestly. Take stock of your credit card balances, interest rates, and monthly payments.

TIPS TO REDUCE CREDIT CARD DEBT

Once you've got a clear picture of where you're at, follow these steps to pay down your debt:

Talk to your credit card company. One simple step you can take is calling your credit card company to negotiate a better deal. Many companies may be willing to reduce your interest rate, waive certain fees, or work out a more manageable repayment plan—especially if you've been a loyal customer or are facing financial hardship. Be prepared to explain your situation clearly and ask directly for a rate reduction or hardship plan. It may not always work, but it's worth the effort and could save you money.

Explore balance transfers. Another potential solution is using a balance transfer card. These cards often offer low or 0% introductory APR on transferred balances for a specific period—usually between 6 and 18 months. By transferring your existing high-interest debt to a card with a lower rate, you can pay off your debt faster since more of your payment goes toward reducing the principal balance—the amount of money you've charged to the card—instead of interest. But beware: Balance transfers usually come with a one-time fee, often around 3% to 5% of the transferred amount. Make sure the savings in interest outweigh the cost of the transfer fee. Also, pay off as much of the debt as possible before the promotional period ends—otherwise, you could end up back in the same cycle.

Consider a personal loan. Unlike credit cards, personal loans typically come with fixed interest rates and fixed monthly payments. They can make budgeting easier and save you money. By consolidating multiple high-interest credit card debts into one personal loan, you may be able to lower your overall interest rate and simplify your repayment process. For example, if you have several credit cards charging interest rates above 20%, consolidating these balances with a personal loan that has a 10% interest rate can help you see significant savings over time. However, this strategy works best if you avoid racking up new debt while paying off the loan. Otherwise, you could end up with more debt than you started with.

Be strategic. Breaking the credit card debt cycle takes time, persistence, and sometimes a combination of strategies. Start by focusing on consistent payments above the minimum to chip away at the balance faster. Consider setting up automatic payments to avoid missed due dates and late fees. It's also important to be honest with yourself about your spending habits, working on them and understanding the root cause of the spending. Reaching out to a nonprofit credit counseling service is a great way to get assistance. They can help you create a personalized debt management plan, negotiate with creditors on your behalf, and offer valuable financial education resources.

PUT IT INTO ACTION:
CREATE YOUR CREDIT CARD DEBT PLAN

Work through these steps to create your own credit card debt plan:

1. **List all your debts.** Write down each credit card you have, the balance owed, the annual percentage rate (APR), and the minimum monthly payments due.

CREDIT CARD	BALANCE	INTEREST RATE	MINIMUM MONTHLY PAYMENT
Total:		Total:	

2. Understand your cash flow. Calculate your monthly income and spending to determine how much you can put toward debt repayment.

3. Prioritize your debts. Decide whether to use the avalanche method (pay off the highest interest debt first) or the snowball method (pay off the smallest balance first).

4. Create a payment plan. Make minimum payments on all debts to avoid penalties. Direct any extra funds toward your prioritized debt.

5. Track your progress. Set a goal date for becoming debt-free. Monitor your balances monthly to celebrate milestones and adjust your plan as needed.

6. Communicate with creditors. Call your credit card company to negotiate a lower interest rate or explore hardship programs if needed.

7. Consider additional strategies. Explore balance transfer cards to lower interest rates (watch for fees). Consider consolidating debt with a personal loan if it offers a lower interest rate.

8. Build new habits. Limit unnecessary spending. Set up automatic payments to ensure you never miss a due date. Regularly review your budget to identify areas where you can spend more intentionally.

Alex Regains Control and Peace of Mind

Alex, a 28-year-old professional, found themself in $15,000 of credit card debt after years of relying on credit to cover living expenses and unexpected costs like car repairs. The high interest rates on multiple cards, averaging around 20%, made it feel like the balance was never shrinking. Alex saw the debt grow despite their efforts because they were only managing the minimum payments.

Alex knew a change was necessary. They began by listing all debts: their balances, minimum payments, and interest rates. After doing some research, Alex chose the avalanche method, focusing on the credit card with the highest interest rate first while contributing minimum payments on the others. To accelerate progress, Alex negotiated a lower interest rate on one card and secured a balance transfer card with a 0% introductory APR for 12 months.

Alex created a budget and tracked their spending to allocate as much as possible toward the transferred balance to make the most of the promotional period. Within two years, Alex paid off all credit card debt and shifted their focus to saving for longer-term goals.

The journey wasn't easy, but with a clear plan and persistence, Alex regained financial control and peace of mind.

CREDIT SCORES AND REPORTS

When you're in school, you take exams and are assigned grades A through F, which are typically converted to the GPA scale. Your **credit score** is basically your "adult GPA." Only this time the score is related to how likely companies are to approve you for a car loan, mortgage, or credit card. Your interest rate is also tied to your credit scores. Potential landlords can review your credit report, and, in some states, employers are allowed to check parts of your credit report to assess your reliability as a potential employee.

Usually, the higher your credit score, the better. A higher credit score can help you negotiate lower interest rates on loans, and decision-makers will see you as a more reliable tenant or employee. It's not necessary at all to obsess over your credit score. (I don't encourage this!) But paying attention to it and checking on your score around once a month can help you see where it stands and if there's any room for improvement.

It's super easy to track down your credit report. Websites like Credit Karma (creditkarma.com) and AnnualCreditReport.com are safe and secure sites to see your credit score and credit report.

HOW TO BUILD A CREDIT SCORE

Not all credit scores are created equal. Just like how grades in school are deemed "very good" or "poor," the same goes for credit scores. The most commonly used credit scoring system in the U.S. is the **FICO score**, created in 1989 by the Fair, Isaac Company (by two dudes name Bill Fair and Earl Isaac).

This is how it breaks down:

CREDIT SCORE RANGE	RATING	DESCRIPTION
800–850	Excellent	Represents the lowest risk; often receives the best terms, interest rates, and credit offers.
740–799	Very Good	Considered a reliable borrower; qualifies for better interest rates and credit options.
670–739	Good	Generally seen as a lower-risk borrower; qualifies for most credit products with decent terms.
580–669	Fair	Considered below average; some lenders may approve credit but with higher interest rates.
300–579	Poor	Indicates a high risk of default; may lead to difficulty obtaining credit or high interest rates.

Your credit score depends on several factors, and not all are weighted the same. Understanding the formula of your credit score can help you take intentional steps to improve and maintain a healthy credit score.

Payment history: Consistently paying off your credit card statements on time shows borrowers that you are a reliable borrower. On the flip side, missed or late payments can negatively impact your score for years. You can consider setting up automatic payments or set a reminder on your phone to pay off your statement, so you don't miss the due date.

Credit utilization: Credit utilization is the percentage of your total available credit that you are currently using. A lower credit utilization is usually better because it shows that you're not overly reliant on borrowed money. A good rule of thumb is to keep your credit utilization below 30%. For example, if you have a total credit limit of $1,000, try to keep your balance under $300. With that said, the most important thing is to pay off your outstanding balance in full each month.

Length of credit history: This considers the age of your oldest account, the age of your newest account, and the average age of all your accounts. For example, if you decide to upgrade to a different credit card, keep your old accounts open (as long as they're in good standing). You will benefit by showing a longer buying history.

Credit mix: Having a diverse mix of credit types, such as credit cards, auto loans, and mortgages, can positively impact your score. It shows that you can manage different types of credit responsibly. However, you don't need to take out new loans just for the sake of building credit (and this is just a small percentage).

New credit requests: When you apply for new credit, lenders can see your credit history, like how many credit card applications you've submitted over the last two years. While having credit (and managing it responsibly) is necessary for building your credit history, it's best not to apply for several lines of credit at a time, as this signals to lenders that you are borrowing too much and overextending yourself. Apply for credit strategically and when necessary. Moderation is key here.

HOW TO READ YOUR CREDIT REPORT

You can think of your **credit report** as a compilation of your personal and financial information and history. It's also used to verify your identity when downloaded by employers or institutions. Once you download your report, here's what you'll see:

Credit Report

- **Personal information:** This section includes your name, date of birth, Social Security number (SSN), current and past addresses, and phone numbers. It also shows variations of your name that have been reported to credit bureaus. Double-check this section to ensure all information is accurate and up to date.

- **Employer history:** This section lists your past and current employers, as reported by lenders. While this may not affect your credit score, it's a part of your identity verification, and you should make sure it reflects accurate and relevant employment details.

- **Credit history:** This is the most important section and details all credit accounts under your name, including credit cards, student loans, mortgages, car loans, and more. You'll see the type of credit, account balances, payment history, status (open or closed), and whether you've missed payments. This history helps creditors determine your reliability when it comes to borrowing and repaying debts.

- **Public records:** This section includes any public financial information like bankruptcies or court judgments. These can have a major negative impact on your credit score and may stay on your report for several years.

- **Credit inquiries:** Every time someone, including you, requests a copy of your credit report, it creates an inquiry. In your report you'll see a list of *hard inquiries* from lenders checking your credit for a loan application. As mentioned before, too many of these can impact your credit score. You'll also see a list of *soft inquiries* from you or potential employer checking your credit. These do not impact your score. Monitoring inquiries can help you avoid unexpected changes in your score.

Checking Up on Your Credit Report

A good rule of thumb is to review your credit report at least once a year to make sure your information looks accurate. Here's what you should look out for:

- Your name, address, and other details are listed correctly

- Recognize all of the listed accounts

- Spot and dispute any inquiries you didn't authorize

If you spot errors, it's a good idea to make a dispute to the credit bureau that generated the report (i.e., Experian, Equifax, or TransUnion). Be prepared with documentation to support your claim: Social Security number, copy of your ID (driver's license or passport), date of birth, and other documents related to your claim.

TAKEAWAYS
THE NEW RULES OF CREDIT AND DEBT

Not all debt is bad, and having debt isn't considered a moral failing—it's more common than you think! That being said, it's never been more important to come up with a plan to tackle your debt and learn best practices when it comes to using credit.

OLD RULES	NEW RULES
Being in debt is something to be ashamed of	Being in debt is a temporary obstacle, not a moral failing
It's my own fault if I end up stuck in debt	Predatory credit practices can lead you into debt, but it's possible to break the cycle
Using a credit card is a necessary milestone to financial independence	Credit cards aren't right for everyone, and they aren't the only way to build your credit score
Rewards cards = free money	Rewards cards are great for perks, but make it easy to rack up serious debt if you're not intentional
Paying off debt is a matter of willpower alone	Willpower alone won't pay down debt; it requires careful strategizing, too

⑥

THE LOWDOWN ON LOANS

The word "loan" can invoke scary feelings in many people. The emotions around loans and money may make some of us so unnerved that you may want to avoid thinking about getting a loan. But unless you are the child of fabulously rich and generous parents (it doesn't hurt to daydream, right?), loans are something you'll likely need to take on at some point if you haven't already.

In the world of finance, a loan is a sum of money that you borrow and agree to pay back over time—with interest. For most people, loans can help you reach big milestones associated with adulting—whether you're borrowing money for college, buying your first car, or dreaming about owning a home. Sure, the idea of owing money to someone can feel like a lot, but loans aren't something to fear. They're tools that, when used wisely, can help you achieve your biggest goals.

The reality is that many people have taken out loans. The better you understand how loans work, the better you can navigate the application and payment processes with confidence. In this chapter, we're breaking it all down. From student loans to car loans to home loans (mortgages), I'll walk you through the essentials, share some personal lessons, and give you the tools to make smart decisions. Let's take the mystery out of loans and turn them into something you can manage with less stress and greater ease.

UNDERSTANDING STUDENT LOANS

If college seems expensive, you're not imagining things. The average student loan debt in the U.S. is now over $38,000. This amount has risen sharply in recent decades—at a much faster rate than average wages have. According to a report from Georgetown University, college costs increased by 169% between 1980 and 2019. Compare that to earnings for workers between the ages of 22 to 27, which have only increased by 19% during that same time period. It's no wonder that student loan forgiveness is such a hot topic in recent years. But while the cost of education remains steep, having a degree can still result in higher earnings over a lifetime, which can make it worthwhile, especially if you make informed choices about taking on a loan.

The type of student loan you choose could save you thousands of dollars. Whether you're heading to college, juggling classes, or figuring out life after graduation, understanding how they work can set you up for success. Let's break down the two main types—federal and private loans—and help you navigate your options with confidence.

FEDERAL LOANS

The most common type of student loan is a **federal loan**, which is offered by the U.S. Department of Education. To learn if you are eligible, fill out the Free Application for Federal Student Aid (FAFSA) at USA.gov/fafsa. This will also show if you can access other assistance like grants, scholarships, and work-study programs.

Federal loans are popular because of their unique benefits, like **fixed interest rates** and **flexible repayment options**. Fixed interest rates mean your payments stay the same over the life of the loan, giving you predictability and making it easier to budget. For example, if you take out a 5% fixed-rate loan, it will stay at 5% no matter what happens to interest rates as the economy goes up and down. There are four main types of federal loans:

- Direct Subsidized Loans

- Direct Unsubsidized Loans

- Direct PLUS Loans

- Direct Consolidation Loans

Here's a cheat sheet to help you quickly compare your options:

LOAN TYPE	WHO CAN BORROW?	WHO PAYS INTEREST DURING SCHOOL?	WHEN INTEREST STARTS
Direct Subsidized	Undergraduates with financial need	Government during school/ grace period	After grace/ deferment periods
Direct Unsubsidized	Undergraduates, graduates, and professional students	Borrower	Immediately after disbursement
Direct PLUS	Graduate/ professional students and parents of dependent undergrads	Borrower	Immediately after disbursement
Direct Consolidation	Any federal student loan borrower	N/A	N/A

Another perk of federal loans is the **grace period**. After graduating, leaving school, or dropping below half-time enrollment, you typically have six months before you need to start making payments. This gives you time to find a job and get settled. Use the grace period to set up a repayment plan or build a small emergency fund to prepare for payments. For subsidized loans, the government covers interest during this period, so your balance doesn't grow. However, unsubsidized loans will continue accruing interest.

Flexible repayment plans make federal loans even more attractive. Options like **income-driven repayment plans adjust** your monthly payments based on your income, making it easier to manage payments during financial ups and downs. Plus, if you qualify, the remaining balances may be forgiven after 20 to 25 years of payments.

PRIVATE LOANS

When federal loans don't cover all your expenses, **private loans** can help fill the gap. They're offered by banks, credit unions, and even some schools. Private loans often have higher borrowing limits and may offer lower interest rates if you or your cosigner has a great credit score. Additionally, private loans typically offer quick approval and flexible terms, such as choosing between fixed and variable interest rates.

But private loans come with some pretty big downsides. They offer fewer borrower protections than federal loans, meaning no income-driven repayment plans or loan forgiveness options. Variable interest rates may rise over time, increasing your costs. Approval is based on your creditworthiness. You may need a cosigner who will become legally responsible for the debt if you can't pay. Private loans often have less flexible repayment terms and can come with additional fees or penalties.

Here's a quick comparison of the pros and cons:

PROS OF PRIVATE LOANS	CONS OF PRIVATE LOANS
✓ Higher borrowing limits	✗ Fewer protections
✓ Potentially lower rates	✗ Variable rates
✓ Flexible terms	✗ Credit-based approval
✓ Quick approval	✗ Less repayment flexibility
✓ Can cover broader expenses	✗ Cosigner risk

Graduate, professional, and international students often find themselves needing private loans when federal options are maxed out. If you're considering private loans, make sure you've fully explored federal aid first since it offers more safeguards and flexibility. Think of federal loans as the dependable, budget-friendly sedan and private loans as the flashy sports car that comes with a hefty price tag—choose wisely!

TIPS FOR REPAYING STUDENT LOANS

The first step in repayment is knowing what you owe. For federal student loans, head to StudentAid.gov and log in with your FSA ID. You'll find all your loan details, including balances, interest rates, and loan services. For private loans, check with your lender directly or review your most recent loan statement. Can't remember all of your loans? You can see your free credit report at AnnualCreditReport.com, and it'll list any private loans in your name.

Once you know what you owe, there are several ways to reduce the cost of your loans. There are a few strategies you can use:

1. **Sign up for automatic repayments:** Set up electronic autopay for your monthly repayments. This helps you pay on time, and most lenders will offer a 0.25% discount on your interest rate. Contact your lender to see if your loan is eligible.

2. **Pay more than the minimum when possible:** Putting in a little extra each month can help lower the total interest you pay over the lifetime of the loan. Be sure to specify that extra payments go toward the principal and not future interest.

3. **Deduct interest on your taxes:** You can deduct up to $2,500 of student loan interest annually from your taxable income to reduce your tax burden and give yourself more room in your budget.

4. **Refinance your loans (with caution):** Refinancing involves trading in your current loans to a new lender for a new loan with more favorable terms. This can help lower your interest rate, but if you refinance federal loans, you'll lose access to benefits like income-driven repayment and loan forgiveness. This option is usually best if you have a private loan and a strong credit history.

What Happens If You Can't Make a Payment?

Once again, federal loans offer some of the most borrower-friendly repayment options, including **deferment** and **forbearance** options. Deferment lets you temporarily pause your payments, and interest doesn't accrue on subsidized loans during this time. Forbearance also pauses or reduces your payments, but interest will continue to build up on all loan types. These options are helpful short-term solutions when money is tight.

You could also consider income-driven repayment plans if your payments feel unmanageable. These plans cap your monthly payments at 10% to 20% of your discretionary income and adjust annually based on changes to your income or family size. After 20 to 25 years of qualifying payments, the remaining balance may even be forgiven, though the forgiven amount might be taxed as income.

For borrowers pursuing careers in public service, Public Service Loan Forgiveness (PSLF) is another great option. Essentially, if you work for the government or a nonprofit and make 120 qualifying payments while employed there, your remaining balance is forgiven tax-free. Teachers working in low-income schools may qualify for forgiveness of up to $17,500, and many states or professions offer their own loan repayment assistance programs as well. There's always help available if you need it—don't hesitate to reach out to your loan servicer or explore your options.

To avoid **delinquency** and **defaulting** on your loans, it's important to stay on top of your monthly payments. A loan becomes delinquent the day after a missed payment. If you don't pay after more than 90 days, your lender will report it to the credit bureaus, potentially damaging your credit score. The consequences of default are even more severe. For federal loans, default typically happens after 270 days of missed payments. When this happens, the entire balance becomes due immediately.

Your credit score will take a major hit, and the government may garnish your wages, seize tax refunds, or withhold Social Security benefits. You'll also lose access to repayment plans and other federal benefits. If you're struggling, it's essential to reach out to your loan servicer right away to explore solutions like deferment, forbearance, or switching to a more affordable repayment plan.

Gen Z Reality Check

As we've seen, student loan costs have shot up in recent decades while our comparative wage growth has slowed. When you add in the financial squeeze from other costs, including car and home loans, Gen Zers are wondering how to keep up. Here's what my community shared.

"As a Gen Zer, one of the biggest challenges around personal finance is managing student debt while trying to save for long-term goals like buying a house or investing."

—Yovela, 23 years old

"[It's] harder for Gen Z to achieve milestones like homeownership and paying off student debt as efficiently as other generations have been able to."

—Emma, 25 years old

"Many are beginning their adult lives burdened with student loan debt, struggling to keep up with the higher cost of living, and often living paycheck to paycheck... Now more than ever, Gen Zers need financial literacy in order to combat today's challenges."

—Natalie, 26 years old

"It's challenging to anticipate the impact of our investments when so much feels unattainable, especially property ownership and building generational wealth from the ground up."

—Jenny, 20 years old

PUT IT INTO ACTION:
TACKLE YOUR STUDENT LOANS

Tackling your student loans effectively starts with understanding where you stand. This quick activity will help you organize your loans, build a repayment plan, and feel more confident about managing your debt.

Step 1: Get the Big Picture

Start by gathering all the information about your student loans in one place. Use the table below to map out the details. For federal loans, visit StudentAid.gov to find your balances and loan servicers. For private loans, check your lender's portal or your credit report.

LOAN TYPE	BALANCE	INTEREST RATE	MONTHLY PAYMENT	LOAN SERVICER
Example: Direct Subsidized Loan	*$5,000*	*4.5%*	*$100*	*Servicer Name*

Step 2: Assess Your Repayment Options

Now that you know what you owe, consider your repayment options:

- Can you afford extra payments? Even small prepayments reduce interest costs.

- Are you struggling with payments? Look into income-driven repayment plans (for federal loans) or refinancing (for private loans).

- Do you qualify for forgiveness? Check programs like Public Service Loan Forgiveness or Teacher Loan Forgiveness.

Write down one or two steps you'll take to improve your repayment strategy:

_____

_____

_____

_____

Step 3: Automate and Stay on Track

If you have a reliable and consistent income, set up automatic payments to reduce the risk of missing deadlines. You could also score an interest rate discount from many lenders. Schedule time every six months to review your repayment progress and adjust your plan if needed.

Jamie Goes from Drowning to Debt-Free

Jamie graduated with a psychology degree and $35,000 in federal student loans. Struggling to find a full-time job right after graduation, she worked part-time at a coffee shop, barely covering rent and expenses. With the six-month grace period coming to an end, Jamie felt overwhelmed by the looming loan payments.

She realized she couldn't just sit there and pretend her loans would magically disappear. Jamie faced them head-on by logging into StudentAid.gov and reviewing her loans. She enrolled in an income-driven repayment (IDR) plan, lowering her monthly payment to $50 based on her income at the time. She signed up for automatic payments to save on interest, which reduced her rate by 0.25%.

After a year, Jamie landed a full-time role as a marketing associate and reevaluated her finances. She created a strict budget to prioritize paying down her student loans and put any extra savings toward them. Jamie also started freelancing on weekends, putting all her extra income into her highest-interest loan. Within three years and thanks to consistent payments, she paid off $25,000 of her balance.

Five years after graduating, Jamie made her final payment and celebrated becoming debt-free. By combining repayment strategies, side income, and discipline, she turned what felt like an impossible debt into a major financial milestone.

YOUR ROAD MAP FOR CAR LOANS

While student loans often represent the first major debt many people encounter, **car loans** are another common financial milestone. My first "big girl" purchase was my Toyota RAV4, which I bought about a year after graduating from college. Having a reliable car was a priority for me, but it also came with a steep learning curve about the car-buying process and how car loans work. Needless to say, I've learned a lot from that experience!

Car loans are a way to finance the purchase of a vehicle when you don't have all the funds to pay for the car up front. Let's say you want to purchase a car that costs $25,000, and you have $5,000 available for a down payment. The loan you need to bring that car home is $20,000—plus interest. The typical length of a car loan can range from 24 months all the way up to 84 months.

Keep in mind that the shorter the loan, the less interest you pay over its lifetime. On the flip side, a longer loan period can reduce monthly payments. But you end up paying more interest. Here's an example to show the difference.

LOAN TERM	INTEREST RATE (APR)	MONTHLY PAYMENT	TOTAL INTEREST PAID	TOTAL LOAN COST
24-month loan	5%	$877	$1,058	$21,058
72-month loan	7%	$341	$4,551	$24,551

As you can see, prolonging the loan by four years costs an extra $3,500—money that could be put toward savings or other financial goals.

HOW TO GET THE BEST CAR LOAN

Taking the time to research car loans can save you thousands of dollars. First, check your credit score. Lenders view borrowers with higher credit scores as less risky, so they offer lower interest rates. If your score needs improvement, work on it before applying for a loan. (Revisit page 113 in Chapter 5 to see how to improve your credit score.)

Next, shop around. Instead of relying solely on dealership financing. Shop and compare loan offers from banks, credit unions, and online lenders. Securing **pre-approval** for a loan can also give you a clear idea of your budget and strengthen your negotiating position at the dealership.

Plan ahead by creating a car savings fund for your down payment. The more cash you put down upfront, the less interest you'll pay over the life of the loan, and your monthly payment will also be reduced.

BEWARE OF HIGH-INTEREST CAR LOANS

High-interest loans are something you want to be careful about when researching your car loan options. Also known as **subprime loans**, these are designed for borrowers with lower credit scores, often coming with interest rates as high as 15% to 25% APR, drastically increasing the total cost of ownership. For instance:

- A $25,000 loan at 5% APR for 60 months will cost $3,306 in interest.

- The same loan at 15% APR will cost $10,684—more than *three times as much!*

Some dealerships, especially "buy here, pay here" locations, use predatory financing tactics to trap borrowers into unfavorable terms. Always read the fine print and avoid loans with high interest rates whenever possible. But if money is tight and you *need* a car, consider buying a used but reliable car that is realistic for your income and overall financial situation. It's not worth it to go into extreme debt over a car, which is ultimately a depreciating asset (something you own that is worth less over time).

LEASING VS. BUYING A CAR

What about leasing a car? Leasing allows you to drive a new car for a fixed term (usually two to three years) with lower monthly payments compared to buying. However, leasing comes with some drawbacks:

- You don't gain ownership of the car

- Mileage limits (e.g., 12,000 miles per year) can lead to costly penalties if exceeded

- Additional fees for wear and tear may apply

Leasing might make sense if you prioritize driving new cars frequently, don't drive much, and are okay with never owning the vehicle. However, for most people, buying a car provides better long-term financial value. For example, for a car with a price tag of $25,000, it may cost $15,000 to lease it for three years—after which time you'll have to return the car. On the other hand, buying the same car allows you to build equity (gain ownership) as you pay off the loan.

TIPS FOR NAVIGATING CAR LOANS

If you're navigating car loans, here are a few actionable steps to make smart decisions:

Check your credit score: Improve it if necessary to qualify for better loan terms.

Set a realistic budget: Factor in not just the monthly payment but the total cost of the loan, including interest. Don't forget about additional costs that can pop up, like repairs and smog checks.

Shop around: Compare offers from at least three lenders to find the best deal.

Plan ahead: Save for a larger down payment to reduce your monthly payments and total interest.

Avoid extras: Say no to unnecessary add-ons like extended warranties or gap insurance unless you've researched their value.

LET'S TALK RENTING VS. BUYING A HOME

Ah, the age-old question: *Should I rent or buy?* Maybe you've been working for a while and saved a decent chunk of money toward a potential home down payment. Most likely the thought has crossed your mind at some point (mine included).

The reality for buying a home these days can be discouraging. The growth of home prices has significantly outpaced wage growth in recent decades. A study by NPR found that in nearly half of metro areas, buyers must make more than $100,000 to afford a median-priced home. To put this into perspective, the median U.S. household income in 2023 was around $80,600.

Our parents—and even social media—tend to glorify homeownership as a marker of success, but the decision to rent or buy isn't always straightforward.

PROS AND CONS OF RENTING VS. BUYING

Renting offers flexibility, lower upfront costs, and fewer responsibilities. In your twenties, it's more common to move around, especially early in your career. If you're unsure about your long-term plans or moving frequently, renting is the better option. You don't have to worry about repairs or paying for extra hidden fees that your own property would require. However, renting means your money is going to a landlord rather than paying off a valuable long-term asset for yourself.

Buying, on the other hand, can build wealth through equity and provide stability and tax benefits. Plus, you get the freedom to personalize your home. That said, it requires an up-front down payment, closing costs, long-term home loan repayments, and ongoing maintenance (e.g., repairing a broken fridge). This adds up to a significant amount of money. Home prices generally appreciate over time. But there's always a risk that market fluctuations could cause the value of a home to become lower than what you paid for, as seen during the 2008 financial crisis.

Deciding What's Right for You

You might've heard people say rent is "throwing money away," but that's not completely true. For many twentysomethings, renting is often the more realistic choice. It gives you the freedom to save, explore your options, and avoid rushing into a financial decision. As a twentysomething myself, I prioritize my ability to move around. By renting, I skipped the added responsibilities of owning a home while saving and investing my money to prepare for when I *am* ready. Buying might make sense if you have a stable income, plan to stay in one place for at least five years, and are prepared for the costs of homeownership.

Ultimately, both renting and buying have their place. The right choice depends on your financial situation, goals, and lifestyle—not anyone else's expectations.

TIPS FOR RENTERS

Navigating the rental market can feel a bit like online dating—exciting at first but filled with potential red flags. Whether you're hunting for your first apartment or looking for a fresh start, the following tips will help you avoid getting caught up in a mess.

Timing matters. When it comes to signing a lease, timing can be everything. Rent prices tend to drop during the off-season (think late fall and winter) when fewer people are moving. You might snag a better deal in December while everyone else is distracted by the holidays. On the other hand, summer is peak rental season (usually when students graduate and move to new cities), and competition can be fierce—like trying to grab the last seat at a Taylor Swift concert.

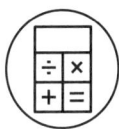

Budget wisely. Consider the **30% rule**: Aim to spend no more than 30% of your gross monthly income (before taxes or deductions) on rent. Of course, this is not a hard and fast rule as it doesn't consider your personal situation, but it's a good benchmark to work from. Factor in additional costs like utilities, renter's insurance, and move-in fees (broker's fee, first and/or last month of rent) to make sure you're not over-stretching yourself financially.

Read the lease carefully. Leases are like terms and conditions—nobody wants to read them, but you really should. Look out for sneaky fees (like pet rent or parking costs), early termination rules, and whether your lease auto-renews or switches to month-to-month after it ends. Your lease is the terms and conditions of your living arrangement. Don't skim this legal contract like when you "agree" to the latest terms and conditions of your latest iPhone update. Read it all the way through.

Negotiate and compare options. Your landlord might not budge on everything, but it never hurts to ask. Can they throw in free parking? Waive move-in fees? Cover utilities? Negotiating might feel awkward, but if it saves money, you'll be glad you did. And always compare multiple options—you wouldn't marry the first person you meet on a dating app, so why settle for the first rental you see?

Save money on moving costs. Moving doesn't have to drain your savings. See if there are creative ways to skirt around pricey moving services. Recruit your strongest friends with the promise of pizza (it works, trust me) to help you move. Go through your stuff and sell your old furniture or other trinkets on Facebook Marketplace. Downsizing your stuff also means fewer boxes to lug around—ask yourself, do you *really* need that stack of old magazines?

SURVIVAL GUIDE FOR LIVING WITH PARENTS

Once you start working, you may dream of living in a plush penthouse apartment of your own. The reality is you may consider moving back home to save money. In fact, nearly half of all young adults ages 18 to 29 still live with their parents, according to an article published by Bloomberg.

After I graduated from UC Berkeley, I also moved back home for a bit. Luckily, my job offer was in the Bay Area, where I'm originally from, so it was a no-brainer for me. Aside from saving on rent, I got to enjoy time with my parents and help them out. And as an only child, I've grown to cherish these moments.

If you're in a similar situation, here are some of my tips to live harmoniously under one roof:

1. Help out around the house. Show your appreciation by pitching in with cooking, cleaning, or whatever needs doing. It's a small way to say thank you and also pick up life skills along the way.

2. Have your own space. Creating some separation and making space for yourself is so important for relaxing and recharging, as in your own room.

3. Discuss expectations. Communicate openly about boundaries, chores, quiet hours, and contributions to ensure everyone's on the same page.

4. Live your life. GO OUTSIDE! Create a routine, whatever that means to you: Go to the office, meet up with friends, or to your favorite workout class. Making space for yourself outside the home helps you maintain other aspects of your life.

IF YOU'RE PLANNING TO BUY A HOME

Buying a home is one of the most significant financial milestones you can experience. It's often considered the pinnacle of the "American Dream." It might feel unrealistic or far away at this point in your life (and that's okay!), but it never hurts to understand how home loans work. This way, you'll be more informed if or when you're ready.

Homeownership can be a powerful way to build wealth. With each repayment of your home loan, you are a small step closer to owning the home (rather than filling up your landlord's wallet). As home values tend to rise over time, you can end up with a big windfall by the time you have paid it off. Meaning, the price you paid for it and the amount you can sell it for may leave you with a very handy profit.

Some people also take on a home loan to buy a rental properly. Put simply, they rent out the property and use the rental income to cover the mortgage while benefiting from any increase in the home's value.

Let's walk through how it all works.

TAKING OUT A HOME LOAN

A **home loan,** or a **mortgage**, is a way for you to purchase a home over time. You will need a **down payment** to secure the home and take out a loan for the remaining amount (just like the process of car loans, as discussed earlier). You must repay the loan over a set number of years along with interest; 30-year mortgages are the most common. The home also serves as collateral, meaning that if you fail to pay back the loan, the lender can take the property and sell it to recoup any of their losses.

So, what do lenders look for when loaning you money for a mortgage? There are a couple of factors they use to determine your eligibility:

- **Credit score:** A higher credit score tells lenders, "Hey, I'm trustworthy!" and can get you lower interest rates. Aim for a score of 700 or above, though some programs accept lower scores. (Return to page 113 in Chapter 5 for more tips on how to increase your credit score.)

- **Down payment:** The down payment is what you bring to the homeowner's table. A 20% down payment of the total price of the home is often required. If you can't meet the 20% threshold you may be charged private mortgage insurance (PMI). It's a fee added by the lender in case you default on your payments. You may be able to find programs that allow you to put down as little as 3% to 5%, but they will likely come with PMI costs. Do what is best for you, but just remember: The more you put down now, the less you pay later.

- **Debt-to-income (DTI) ratio:** This fancy-sounding term just means lenders want to make sure your debts don't outweigh your paycheck. A DTI of 36% or lower is the sweet spot. For example, if your gross monthly income is $5,000, aim to keep total monthly debt payments under $1,800.

- **Stable income:** Lenders love predictability, and a steady job history is a giant green flag. Bonus points if you have a financially solid co-borrower to back you up.

MAKING SENSE OF MONTHLY REPAYMENTS

When it comes to mortgages, the monthly payment can feel like a mystery. But fear not! Let's break it down here to save you opening 47 tabs on your browser. Here's what typically makes up that monthly bill.

Principal and Interest

Think of this as the "meat and potatoes" of your mortgage payment. The **principal** is the money you actually borrowed to buy your home, while the **interest** is what you pay the lender for the ability to borrow that money. Here are two of the main mortgage types you can consider:

- **Fixed-rate mortgages** are like a reliable friend who never changes plans on you—your interest rate stays the same for the life of the loan.

- **Adjustable-rate mortgages (ARMs)**, on the other hand, start off with a lower rate but can change over time. It's like that trendy cafe that seems affordable at first until you realize that you've paid an extra five dollars for oat milk.

Property Taxes

Every homeowner's favorite surprise! **Property taxes** are charged by your local government to pay for things like parks, roads, and public transport. They're often bundled into your mortgage payment. Your lender usually sets aside a chunk of your payment into an escrow account (basically a savings jar they manage) to cover taxes when they're due. Think of it as outsourcing your tax worries—except you're still footing the bill. Depending on the specific lender's policies, there may be associated costs related to maintaining the escrow account. Property taxes can vary wildly depending on where you live. For a $300,000 home in Texas, you might pay $6,000 annually, while the same home in Colorado might cost you $2,000.

Homeowners Insurance

Homeowners insurance isn't just a "nice-to-have"—your lender requires it. It protects you from life's curveballs, like theft or a rogue tree branch deciding to remodel your roof. The cost is included in your monthly payment, so you won't forget to pay it. However, you can also pay for insurance separately, which gives you more flexibility and control over your insurance payments. Plus, paying it annually instead of monthly might save you on fees.

Condo or HOA Fees

If you're living in a condo or a community with a **Homeowners Association (HOA),** you'll likely have extra fees for things like landscaping, pool maintenance, or that fancy security gate that never seems to work. These fees aren't technically part of your mortgage, but they're worth factoring into your budget so they don't catch you off guard.

Here's a sample breakdown of a monthly mortgage payment:

Sample Monthly Mortgage Breakdown

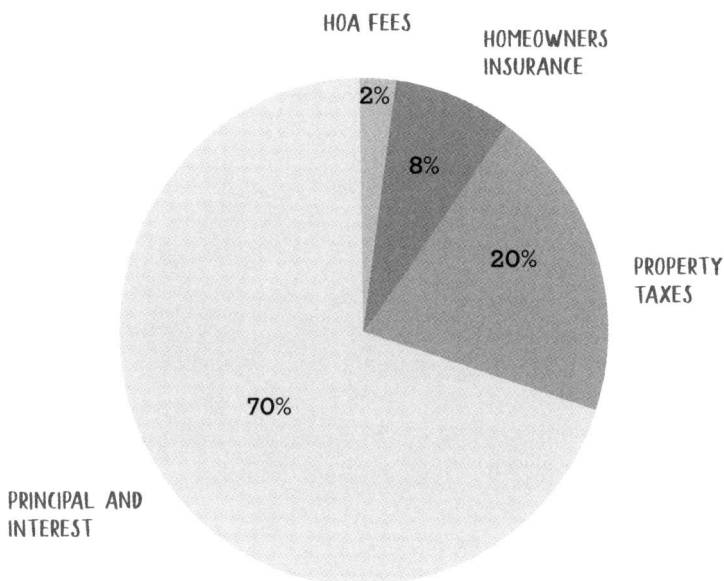

In the U.S., there are a couple of programs that help make purchasing a home more accessible if you fall into certain categories.

- **FHA loans:** With as little as 3.5% required for a down payment, these loans are ideal for first-time buyers with limited savings or lower credit scores. For example, an FHA loan might allow a first-time buyer to purchase a $200,000 home with just $7,000 down instead of $40,000 for a conventional loan.

- **VA loans:** These loans are available to veterans and active-duty military and often require no down payment and have competitive interest rates.

- **USDA loans:** Low-interest loans to buyers in rural and suburban areas, with no down payment required.

- **First-time homebuyer assistance:** Many states offer grants or tax credits to help with down payments and closing costs. Check with your state's policies to see exact terms and how to apply.

Risky Mortgage Moves

Here are some other things to consider avoiding when it comes to taking out a mortgage:

Making a small down payment: While low down payments (for example, 5% instead of 20%) can make homeownership more accessible, they often result in higher monthly payments and the added cost of PMI (page 138). PMI does make affording a home more accessible, but make sure you run the numbers to see if your monthly payment makes sense for your budget.

Borrowing too much: Your dream home shouldn't leave you eating instant ramen for dinner every night for years on end. Stick to what fits your budget comfortably and avoid becoming "house-rich, cash-poor" (aka "house-poor").

Ignoring fees: Watch out for hidden costs like closing fees, origination fees, and prepayment penalties. These can add thousands to your expenses.

Borrowing against your home: Using your home as collateral (e.g., through a home equity loan) can be risky. If you can't repay, you risk losing your property.

Skipping a home inspection: Always invest in a professional home inspection to avoid expensive surprises like structural issues or outdated electrical systems.

TAKEAWAYS
THE NEW RULES OF LOANS

Taking out a loan is a big commitment, but it can be a useful tool to achieve your life goals, whether it's funding your education or getting your first home or car. Everyone is on their own path when it comes to these milestones, so take your time to do your research and decide what's best for you.

OLD RULES	NEW RULES
Buy a home as early as you can to achieve financial security	Buying a home isn't as easy as it used to be and doesn't have to be a first step to financial security
Renting is throwing away your money	Renting is a great way to enjoy flexibility and move around in your twenties
Living at home with family in your twenties is embarrassing	It's okay and increasingly normal for people in their twenties to live at home while they save
Stick to minimum repayments for loans	Fast-track loan repayments to get closer to your long-term goals
Taking out loans is a sign you can't manage your money	Loans are a financial tool. When used wisely, they can help you achieve important life goals

7

INVESTING LIKE A PRO

O ne of the most common misconceptions about investing is that you need to be "rich" or have a lot of money to start investing. But that couldn't be *further* from the truth. You can start investing with as little as ten dollars and your phone.

Investing in the stock market is one of the most accessible ways for anyone, like you and me, to build wealth without any high barrier to entry. However, it's too often framed as an overly complex topic. There are so many resources and conflicting viewpoints that figuring out where to start can feel overwhelming.

In this chapter, we'll break down all the basics you need to know about investing, from the various types of accounts to how to make your first investment. I'll also explain the best ways to invest in your retirement funds. By the end of the chapter, you'll walk away with more confidence in navigating the investing world.

THE BASICS OF INVESTING

No doubt you've heard of the **stock market**, right? But maybe you aren't completely clear about what the stock market is and does. Not a problem!

This analogy may help. Let's say you're opening a bakery business. To start the bakery, you need funding, so you ask your friends to invest in your business. In exchange, your friends each receive a small bit of your business, a **share**, which makes them part-owners of the bakery. Imagine a giant meeting where people can trade these shares on a much larger scale. Essentially, that's the stock market in a nutshell.

So, how does this play out in the real world? A company has stock, and they are sold as shares. Stocks refer to the broad ownership of a company, while shares refer to the specific number of ownership units, or **equity**, in a company. For example, if someone says, "I invest in stocks," it means they own equity in a company or companies, but it doesn't specify the amount. On the other hand, if someone says, "I own ten shares of Google," it specifies the exact amount of ownership they have in that particular company. The amount you pay for a single share is known as the **stock price**.

Let's say there is a business called Company X, and you want to buy a share of this company. For this example, its stock price is $100, so you place an order to purchase one share. You now own a tiny fraction of Company X. If the company does well, more people are likely to buy shares, pushing up the stock price. If it performs poorly, more people are likely to sell their shares, pushing the price down. If the stock price of Company X rises to $200 and you sell your share at that price, you make a $100 profit (before tax), also known as a **capital gain**.

The modern U.S. stock market we know today started in 1792 when the New York Stock Exchange (NYSE) was established in New York City, only 16 years after the United States was founded. There was a famous tree called the Buttonwood Tree, where 24 stock traders signed the Buttonwood Agreement, outlining the guiding principles of stock trades based on existing European trading systems at the time. The Nasdaq is another stock exchange, founded in 1971, specializing mainly in technology and growth-oriented stocks. The stock market and stock exchanges are related but are two distinct concepts. A stock exchange is a specific marketplace for trading, while the stock market is the aggregate of all trading activity.

Stock trading used to occur physically in person. The typical image in the 1980s was of suited-up finance bros feverishly pointing at big screens and yelling "buy!" and "sell!" into their telephones. But with modern technology, most stock trading occurs online (except for a few in-person exceptions like on the NYSE trading floor), and pretty much anyone can participate, as long as they have an internet connection and money to invest.

It's never been easier to open your own online **investment account**, sometimes called a "brokerage account." This account acts like a digital wallet when you want to buy and sell assets on the stock market. When you log into your investment account, you can invest in thousands of companies and funds. Some of the biggest companies you can buy stocks in include Apple, NVIDIA, Google, Meta, Amazon, and many more. We'll talk more about figuring out what to invest in later in this chapter.

Investing isn't just the stuff of movies. It has a real purpose. Investing in assets like stocks can help you grow your money and build long-lasting wealth. Through investing, you can reach your financial goals and eventually have enough funds to retire. Each year, inflation causes the value of your money to decrease, meaning the same dollar can buy less over time. By investing, your money has the potential to grow at a rate that outpaces inflation, helping you maintain or even increase its purchasing power.

Gen Z Reality Check

Not sure where to start with stocks? Or how best to invest for retirement? Maybe you know the basics of investing and tried to do your own research on YouTube and social media. Did you encounter those fast-talking finance gurus who left you more confused than when you began? You're not alone, as the comments from my community below reveal. But fear not; this chapter has everything you need to know to invest wisely.

> "A lot of the advice out there is about how to save, but there's no one telling you what to do with the money you've saved! I just started a new job, and it's so hard to decide where to put all the money I've earned."
>
> —Ryan, 23 years old

> "I find it really hard to gauge what type of investments I should be making. Roth 401(k) vs. traditional 401(k)? Should I invest in the stock market?"
>
> —Angelina, 20 years old

> "It becomes overwhelming thinking about...whether you're investing enough or too little, and if you're actually making progress with your funds when you invest. Sometimes it feels like I have decision paralysis."
>
> —Jade, 25 years old

TYPES OF INVESTMENTS

Now you know the basics of investing, let's go over the most common types of investments you can start investing in and what they mean.

INVESTING IN STOCKS

Earlier, you learned that a company's stock is sold in **shares**, which people buy and sell in the **stock market**. Anyone can trade shares if they have a brokerage account and funds to invest.

Let's look at another analogy to help explain more about how investing in stocks works. Imagine you're going shopping for your weekly grocery run. The supermarket represents the stock market, where you can buy and sell stocks similar to picking out various food items on the shelves. Just like a shopper looking for a good deal, you're an investor looking to invest in stocks that will provide you with the best returns.

Stocks, also called shares, are company pieces you can buy. However, you can only buy stocks from publicly traded companies. Think Google, Apple, Amazon, etc. As we've discussed earlier, picking individual stocks to invest in is very time-consuming, and there's high risk involved—the possibility of higher growth and losses. In other words, the value of the stock (the stock price) can go up or down over time. For example, when Amazon's stock price was first rising in the early 2000s, people were also investing in other promising new companies, like Pets.com and eToys. If you were lucky enough to invest in Amazon and hold onto your shares, you'd have made a lot of money now. But you'd be left with nothing if you invested in those other companies, which have since gone bust.

INVESTING IN FUNDS

Investing in funds is the other, often safer, alternative to stocks. These are baskets of stocks that have already been curated for you. The main reason why funds are attractive to investors is due to **diversification**. Instead of investing in a single stock, by investing in a fund, you are investing in many stocks at the same time, which reduces your overall risk. Funds are usually the foundation of a stable investment portfolio, especially if you're investing for the long term and into retirement.

Let's review the possible options.

Mutual Funds

One option is investing in a **mutual fund**. Think of mutual funds as a pre-packed grocery basket offered by the supermarket. Instead of picking individual items (stocks), you buy a pre-made basket created by an expert (a fund manager). This basket has a mixture of items tailored to a specific goal, such as healthy eating (stock diversification within a particular category). The basket's contents are fixed for the day, and you can buy them only at the market's closing time. Mutual funds are priced at the end of each trading day. Most are actively managed, meaning the fund manager is constantly researching and switching out stock holdings to optimize the fund's performance.

On the other hand, when a fund is passively managed, the fund's goal is to match the performance of an index. The main downside of mutual funds is their high fees in exchange for active management. Additionally, most mutual funds don't end up outperforming the market.

Exchange-Traded Funds and Index Funds

Another type of fund you can invest in is **exchange-traded funds** or **ETFs**. They are similar to mutual funds; they're only traded like stocks, and you can buy and sell them at any point during the open trading window. ETFs can either be actively or passively managed, but most are passive investments following the performance of a particular index, for example, the S&P 500 or Nasdaq 100.

Speaking of passive investments, that's where **index funds** come in. Unlike mutual funds, where fund managers are actively trying to beat the market, index funds aim to match the performance of an index. To make sense of this, using the supermarket analogy, instead of paying for a fancy curated basket that matches only certain people's tastes (actively managed mutual funds), you go with the reliable, budget-friendly option that is a bestseller and mimics what everyone else is buying (passive index funds).

As mentioned earlier, index funds that track the S&P 500 (the top 500 companies in the U.S.) have a historical annual performance of 6% to 7%, adjusted for inflation. Index funds are especially significant if you want to "set it and forget it." You can purchase shares of the fund and ensure it tracks the market performance without doing additional work to manage what's going on with your investments. For most people, index funds are the simplest and most cost-effective way to invest in a diversified portfolio. Remember: All index funds are mutual funds, but not all mutual funds are index funds. This distinction is important because it helps investors understand the difference in fees, management style, and potential returns.

ETFs and index funds that are passively managed have lower **expense ratios**, which is a fee that you pay on an automatic basis annually to own the fund in your portfolio. The lower the expense ratio, the better. An expense ratio below 0.10% is considered low, so make sure you do your research on expense ratios when looking at funds.

Let's talk about specific examples of ETFs and index funds that track the S&P 500. When you log into your brokerage account, you need to type in what's called the "ticker symbol" of a fund or ETF. This tells the brokerage what fund you are looking to buy (or sell).

The examples of ETFs and index funds that follow are managed by Vanguard, which is a major brokerage. You may see similar funds from other brokerages or firms like Fidelity and Schwab. They have different ticker symbols to track the same index, but they typically serve the exact same purpose.

- *VTI:* This ticker symbol is short for Vanguard Total Stock Market Index Fund ETF. Since this is an ETF, you can trade this at any time during the market open trading window. There is no initial minimum amount you must buy. You can buy any quantity you want, even **fractional shares**, which is when you purchase a portion of a share instead of a full share. Many brokerages offer the option to buy fractional shares, but if not, you'd need to buy a full share.

- *VTSAX:* The full name is Vanguard Total Stock Market Index Fund Admiral Shares. This is the index fund example of VTI, and it does the *exact* same thing, tracking the S&P 500. The main differences are: (1) your account will buy the price of the fund that day at the end of the trading day, and (2) there is a $3,000 initial minimum (for this specific fund).

INVESTING IN BONDS

Bonds are another type of investment that is considered lower risk than stocks. When you buy a bond, you are essentially acting as a bank, lending out money to a borrower, like the government or a company, at a fixed interest rate for a certain amount of time. In return for lending out your money, the organization or entity that is on the other end of the bond pays you interest. Bond prices are inversely correlated to interest rates set by the federal government. When interest rates go up, bond prices go down, and vice versa.

You can buy bonds through a brokerage, similar to how you would buy a stock. You can also buy them directly through a government website like TreasuryDirect.gov. Bonds are a more stable investment that preserves your money compared to the aggressive growth that you'd get from stocks. Having some bonds can be a good way to diversify your investment portfolio, but it doesn't make sense to include many bonds if you're in your twenties and

thirties. When you're younger, it's ideal to focus on stock investments for more aggressive growth and introduce more bonds into
your portfolio as you get older for capital preservation.

BUT ISN'T INVESTING LIKE GAMBLING?

Some people view investing in the stock market as if it is as risky
as placing all your chips on a roulette table at a casino. Maybe
you've seen news headlines of cryptocurrency "pump and dump"
schemes. That's when fraudsters share false positive information
about an asset to inflate its value, then dump their holdings at its
peak before the value crashes. They do this with the hopes that
they get more money for the sale, often at the expense of others.
While these things do happen, it's worth considering the bigger
picture.

**The goal of investing isn't to get rich tomorrow; it's to invest
for the long-term future.** I like to think of investing in the stock
market as a "get rich slow" and not a "get rich tomorrow" scheme.
Some people get nervous when they see the value of their investments drop in the short term and tend to sell off their investments.
Remember, money is inherently emotional; you might feel pan-
icked or upset when your investments go down on a "red day"
(when the stock market is down). However, the ultimate goal of
investing is to build long-term, sustainable wealth, not to get rich
the next day. There's short-term volatility, but when you zoom out
on how the market performs over time, that's where the big growth
happens.

**Most people will not find success by "betting" on individual
stocks.** Even some professionals who research and actively pick
stocks for a living have trouble beating the stock market's average
returns. And that holds true over 20 years. The average, everyday
person does not have the tools to select stocks that will beat the
market long-term successfully. Sure, there might be cases where

you hit a home run from buying one stock. But that's usually more about luck. Over time, achieving an average return from your stock market investments is normal—and a good thing. This can be done by investing in low-cost index funds that track the growth of the overall market, like the S&P 500, both of which we will go into detail in the following few sections.

Yes, there will always be a degree of risk in investing—but no risk, no reward! For example, the market is usually volatile. This means the price moves up and down from day to day, year to year, and sometimes hour to hour. But over the long term, the ups far outpace the downs. Think of investing in the market as investing in the overall U.S. economy—your investments grow with it as the economy grows. When done wisely, investing is a safe way to build long-term wealth.

If you remember from Chapter 3, when you begin to save money, you should first set up an emergency fund (page 61) to be ready for life's curveballs. Once you've done that, the next step is to invest extra cash for the long haul.

WHAT IS CRYPTOCURRENCY?

Bitcoin this, Ethereum that—these are some of the most common buzzwords thrown around when it comes to **cryptocurrency**, or **crypto** for short. Bitcoin and Ethereum are the two biggest forms of digital currency that run on blockchain, a secure, decentralized ledger shared across many computers. Blockchain stores information (like transactions) in blocks that are linked together in a chain, making it nearly impossible to tamper with since every computer on the network has access to the same data. Crypto uses a secret language that protects data, called "cryptography," to secure transactions and verify the creation of new coins. Most cryptocurrencies are not controlled by a central authority like a bank or government. So there's very limited regulation in this space. Bitcoin, invented in 2008, was the first cryptocurrency, and since then, the crypto space has exploded in popularity.

A large part of the crypto hype has been driven by Gen Z. In fact, it's actually the most common investment we make. Largely driven by success stories on social media and easier access to investing, many Gen Zers find crypto to be appealing because of its potential for quick gains and feelings of FOMO (fear of missing out).

Because there's so little regulation in the space, crypto is a breeding ground for scams and risks. It's not uncommon to see investors fall into traps and get completely wiped out overnight. There's no such thing as "get rich quick." If somebody claims otherwise, run.

If you're interested in crypto, make sure to do thorough research and use reputable platforms. Experts recommend keeping crypto a small percentage (no more than 3%) of your overall investment portfolio to manage risk.

ONLINE INVESTING SLANG

With the rise of digital finance, it's never been easier to start investing your own funds. Here are some terms or traps that you're likely to come across if you enter the world of online investing:

Bullish: A bullish investor is someone who believes their asset will rise in value (compared to a "bearish" investor, who is pessimistic about an investment).

DYOR: An acronym for "do your own research," DYOR means to carefully investigate anything you want to invest in before putting your money at risk.

Robo-advisor: A robo-advisor uses algorithms and software to manage your investments with little to no human input.

Rug pull: When a scammer creates a cryptocurrency and persuades people to invest, then suddenly sells their holdings, leaving investors with worthless holdings.

Meme stock: Any stock that gains sudden popularity and hype through sites like Reddit and social media, which leads to a sudden increase in its stock price.

Micro-investing: Taking very small sums of money—the digital equivalent of spare change in your pocket—and regularly investing these amounts to slowly build a bigger portfolio.

THE MAGIC OF COMPOUND INTEREST

The following section covers compound interest, which is by far the most potent force a young person has when investing. Albert Einstein reportedly once said, "Compound interest is the eighth wonder of the world. He who understands it earns it; he who doesn't pays it."

In the simplest terms, compound interest is about earning interest on your interest. It's kind of like a snowball rolling down a hill. It starts small, but as it picks up speed, the snowball becomes bigger and bigger.

Here's another way to think about the stock market. It's from a well-known folktale from India. It's about a girl who outsmarts a greedy king who hoards rice during a famine. The girl does a good deed and is allowed to speak to the king. She presents him with a seemingly simple request: Give her one grain of rice, doubled daily for 30 days. He agrees.

So, on day two, she gets two grains, and on day three, she gets four grains. This is repeated for 30 days. By the end of the month, the king gives her over 500 million grains of rice. The king's stash of rice is depleted, as the girl tricked him into giving it away and feeding the entire country.

Of course, our money doesn't double from investment gains yearly (though I wish it did). However, the same principle applies; while growth might feel slow initially, you can see the effects of compounding at an exponential rate over time.

This is why investing for your future as early as possible is essential. The time value of money is particularly valuable when you're young because you have more time to build wealth and let compound interest run on autopilot. If you start investing at age 20, you have 45 years of compound interest until age 65, but if you start investing at age 35, you have 30 years of compound interest. That's 15 years of missed gains in the market.

Money is cheaper when you're young. If you're reading this and you feel behind, don't panic. The best time to invest was yesterday, but today is the next best time to invest.

COMPOUND INTEREST IN THE STOCK MARKET

You can see compound interest over time in the **S&P 500**, which stands for the Standard and Poor's 500. It was fully established in 1957 and is a stock market index (for more on indexes, see page 150) that tracks the performance of 500 of the largest companies listed on stock exchanges in the U.S. The index is rebalanced quarterly, and companies can be added or removed, so companies need to adhere to specific guidelines to stay in the "club."

Historically, the S&P 500 has grown by 10% a year over the last 20 years, or around 6–7% when adjusted for inflation. That might not seem like much to be excited about, but it's a few percentage points more than the growth of a high-yield savings account, which might only grow your money by 4% (or even less, depending on the interest rates set by the Fed). Being "average" usually gets a bad rap, but when it comes to the stock market, it's a great thing!

When you invest in the S&P 500, you're essentially investing in the growth of the entire U.S. economy. The U.S. is constantly innovating and creating new products, so the S&P 500 is typically an indicator of positive growth.

INVESTING YOUNG: A TALE OF TWO FRIENDS

Investing while you're young can make a huge difference in your investment portfolio. Let's use an example of two friends, Natalie and Zach. Natalie learned about investing early and tried to convince Zach to do the same. But Zach wasn't having it and told his friend, "I have so much time. It's too early to worry about investing. I'll catch up on it later. Plus, I want to enjoy my twenties before worrying about all that 'adult' stuff."

Natalie and Zach both had the time, but Natalie decided to use her youth to her advantage. She was 20 years old, still in college, and didn't have much disposable income to invest, so she started by investing $100 a month into a low-cost index fund that tracks the S&P 500. For the sake of this example, let's assume that Natalie continues to invest $100 a month until she is 65 years old, and that the S&P 500 continues to grow at 10% a year. She will end up with $869,975 while only contributing a total of $54,100.

Zach finally started to prioritize investing later in life at age 35. He realized Natalie had been in the game for 15 years already but thought, "I'll contribute more per month than her, and I'll catch up." Zach puts in an initial contribution of $5,000 and continues to invest $200 a month, double the amount of Natalie. At age 65, Zach only has a balance of $482,033, but he contributed $77,000 of his own money. He ends up with a lower balance than Natalie, even though he contributed more than her.

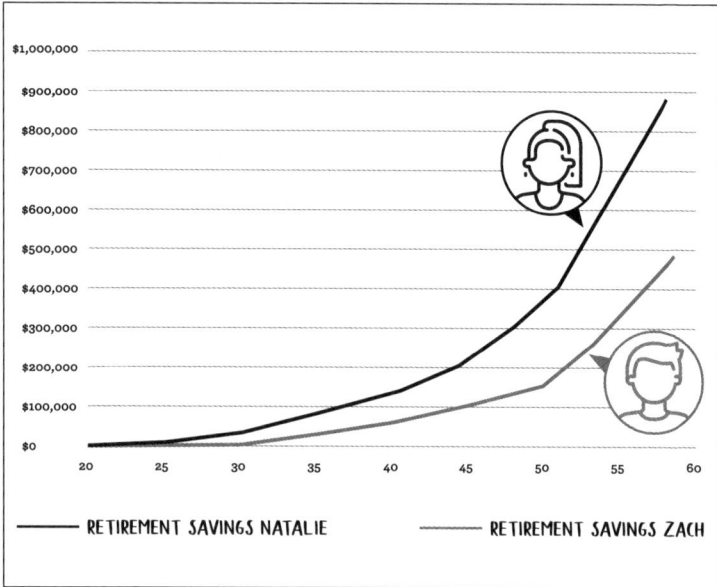

20	25	30	35	40	45	50	55	60

——— RETIREMENT SAVINGS NATALIE   -------- RETIREMENT SAVINGS ZACH

This graphic shows another important point: You don't need much money to start investing. For Natalie, it was $100 a month. You can gradually build future wealth by investing a small amount consistently over a long period. Plus, starting early helps you get into the habit and practice of investing and prioritizing your future self.

Should You Be Debt-Free Before Investing?

Compound interest is your friend when growing your savings and investments. But it can also work in reverse by compounding the interest on debt, making it harder to pay off if you leave it for an extended period of time. Some types of debt compound much faster than high-yield savings accounts or the S&P 500 grow.

For example, the average credit card interest rate is 24% and is compounded daily, meaning interest is added to the total balance daily. If left ignored, credit card debt can snowball into an unfathomable amount. By paying off credit card debt, you get an immediate 24% return on your funds because your income's not going away to interest. If you have credit card debt, I suggest flipping back to page 96 in Chapter 5 for tips on paying this off before you consider investing.

The math is more nuanced regarding other forms of debt, like student loans or mortgages, which often have lower interest rates. Typically, prioritize putting your income toward debt with an interest rate of 6% or greater. If it's less than that, the debt doesn't necessarily need to be fully paid off before you start investing. You could consider a balanced approach where you split your money between paying off debt monthly and investing the rest. But everyone's situation is unique, so evaluate how the math works out for your situation and if investing now makes sense or if you need to prioritize paying off some of the debt first.

TIPS FOR INVESTING

When it comes to researching stocks or funds you want to invest in, you have several tools at your disposal. Brokerages like Fidelity, Vanguard, and Schwab have detailed stock investment research tools that break down news, performance, stats, and ratings for stocks, funds, bonds, money market funds, and more. They also include buy-and-sell rating reports from reputable investment research firms like Morningstar and CFRA. I find these research portals to be a lot more comprehensive compared to other sites, but Google Finance and Yahoo Finance are also excellent sources for a more simplified view.

Do your own research. If you're interested in studying individual company finances and stocks more closely, I recommend learning about key metrics like price-to-earnings (P/E) ratio, dividend yield, and return on equity (ROE) to make more informed decisions. But if you're more of a lazy investor who buys and holds index funds (and there's nothing wrong with that!), this is not totally necessary.

Beware of fees. Watch out for fees when it comes to investments. For example, mutual funds and ETFs charge expense ratios, which are annual fees expressed as a percentage of your investments. Active mutual funds have higher fees while passive index funds have the lowest expense ratios, giving you more money back in your pocket. Additionally, some brokerages charge commissions (fees) for buying or selling stocks. The biggest brokers like Fidelity, Schwab, Vanguard, and Robinhood offer commission-free trades.

Consider dividends. A **dividend** from a stock is a payment from a company when you own a share of its stock, typically distributed quarterly. Not every stock has a dividend. Some stocks and funds have Dividend Reinvestment Plans (DRIP). This means you can automatically reinvest the dividends back into your total holding of that investment. Reinvesting your dividends allows you to continuously benefit from compound interest; now you have more shares in the investment, so you earn dividends from the dividends.

Invest what you can regularly. You may have heard of the phrase "time in the market beats timing the market." Don't deliberately wait for the market to go down before you invest. Make sure to invest equal amounts of money at consistent intervals. Either bi-weekly or monthly means you spread out your risk and lower the average cost of your shares over time. You also develop the good habit of investing regularly.

Consider ethical investing. This is another area to explore for those who are looking to align their personal values with what they invest in, while achieving good returns. It's gained popularity in recent years, especially among Gen Zers, who are generally more concerned about issues like climate change and social inequality than previous generations. You can consider environmental, social, and governance (ESG) funds, which select companies that treat the planet and their employees well. A more specific form of ethical investment is a socially responsible investing (SRI) fund. It takes it a step further from ESG funds by adding or removing companies based on ethical considerations, for example, avoiding tobacco, alcohol, or weapons production. Make sure to do your own research to see which funds align with your values.

THE INVESTMENT RISK LADDER

We've looked at a lot of info about investing so far, but how do all these types of investments stack up against one another in terms of how risky they are (or aren't)? This visual should help guide you, with investments ranked from lowest to highest risk.

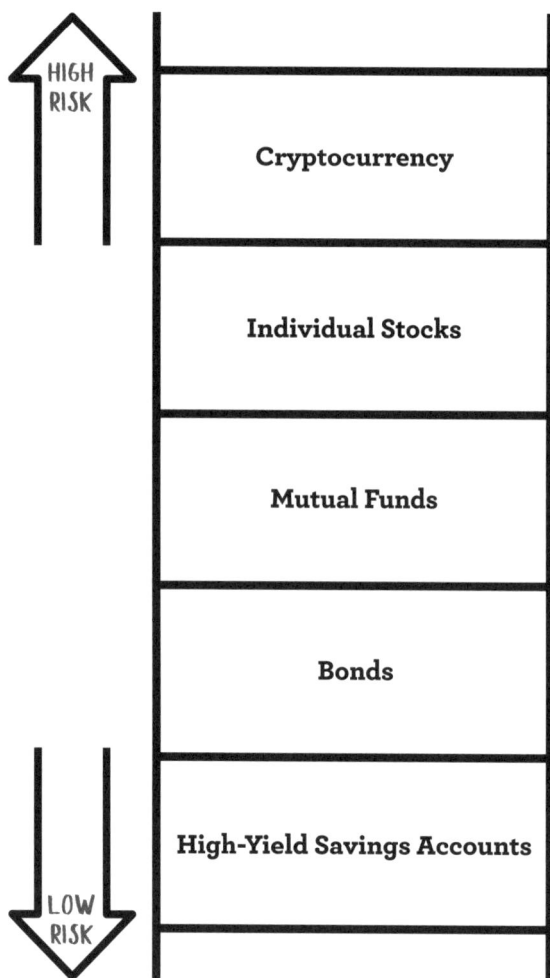

HIGH RISK

Cryptocurrency

Individual Stocks

Mutual Funds

Bonds

High-Yield Savings Accounts

LOW RISK

PUT IT INTO ACTION:
WHAT KIND OF INVESTOR ARE YOU?

Investing isn't one-size-fits-all. Discover your unique financial personality with this quick quiz that reveals your investment style, risk tolerance, and potential strategy:

1. What is your primary goal for investing?

a) Grow my wealth over the long term

b) Generate steady income

c) Save for a specific short-term goal

d) Preserve my savings with minimal risk

2. How would you react if your investments dropped 20% in value?

a) Hold steady and wait for the market to recover

b) Reassess and possibly adjust my investments

c) Feel worried but stick to my plan

d) Pull out my investments immediately

3. How long do you plan to keep your money invested?

a) 10+ years—I'm thinking about my future self

b) 5–10 years—long enough to see meaningful growth

c) 2–5 years—I've got some big milestones coming up

d) Less than 2 years—I might need the money sooner

Continued >

4. What level of risk are you comfortable with?

a) High risk for potentially high rewards

b) Moderate risk with a balance of growth and safety

c) Low risk for slow and steady returns

d) Minimal risk—I can't afford to lose money

5. How involved do you want to be in managing your investments?

a) I love learning and want to actively manage my portfolio

b) I'm interested but prefer a mix of hands-on and automated options

c) I'd rather stick to simple, low-maintenance strategies

d) I want everything to be automated

Results:

- **Mostly As:** You're a growth-oriented investor. Consider high-growth options like stocks or index funds and focus on long-term gains.

- **Mostly Bs:** You value balance. Explore a mix of stocks, bonds, and ETFs to diversify your portfolio.

- **Mostly Cs:** You prioritize stability with some growth. Look into low-risk funds and conservative investments.

- **Mostly Ds:** You're cautious and likely focusing on saving versus investing. Focus on safe options like high-yield savings accounts, money market funds, or CDs.

Priya Becomes a Confident Investor

When Priya graduated college at age 22, she felt totally lost when it came to investing. She'd heard of terms like "index funds" and "compound interest" but was overwhelmed by the volume of information out there. However, she realized from talking to mentors and researching online that it's essential to start investing early.

She began by seeking out resources like personal finance books, blogs, and YouTube channels that focus on breaking down investment strategies for beginners. Rather than diving into her brokerage account without much prior knowledge, Priya spent a few weeks learning the basics: understanding the difference between stocks, bonds, and ETFs, plus researching terms like "expense ratios" and "risk tolerance."

Once she felt more confident, Priya opened a brokerage account that offers commission-free trades. She set a goal to invest 15% of her monthly income and automated contributions to a low-cost total market index fund. Within a year of consistently investing, Priya began to see her investments grow.

By starting small and sticking to her plan, she gained the assurance that investing wasn't as intimidating as she once thought it to be. Priya also made sure to spend a little bit of time each morning to catch up on the market news. She slowly gained confidence as she became more knowledgeable in this area. Today, Priya is a proud advocate for financial literacy and encourages her peers to take their first step toward investing and taking care of their future selves.

INVESTING YOUR RETIREMENT SAVINGS

I opened my first investment account, which happened to be a retirement account, a Roth IRA, when I was 20 years old. I had made some money from an internship and knew that saving for retirement was important. I didn't quite grasp the importance of starting early until a bit later.

"But Lillian, retirement seems like ages away. Why should I care about saving for retirement when I have barely started my adult life?"

This was my initial thought as well. I was fed the narrative that your twenties should be for fun and investing for retirement wasn't something to worry about until I was older and made substantially more money. But boy, was I wrong.

Even though the concept of retirement might seem far away, the earlier you start investing, the more time you have for your money to compound (refer back to the section "The Magic of Compound Interest"). Most people in their twenties don't have other significant expenses to worry about, like a mortgage and dependents. It's the perfect time to set aside a small amount every month toward retirement. It's easier to save a little every month than trying to play catch up during your later years. A target guideline to follow is saving 10% to 15% of your income for retirement. Investing in my retirement early in my twenties was one of the best financial decisions I've made. I established a solid investment foundation that will have the opportunity of decades of market compounding.

Once you retire from the workforce, you no longer have a salary and instead have to live off of savings, retirement income, or government programs. In the U.S., the median age for retirement is 62, and the median retirement savings for someone between 55 to 64 is $185,000. There could be many factors for retiring earlier or later than the traditional retirement age of 67, including financial, health, and lifestyle factors. "Traditional retirement age" here refers to the age you are eligible to receive full Social Security benefits.

401(K)S

At your job, you've likely come across a **401(k)** when reviewing your company's benefits offerings. They let you contribute
toward your retirement directly out of your paychecks. Back in
the old days, companies rewarded loyal employees by providing
them with pensions, so the employer took on the burden of
saving for their employees' retirements. However, pensions no
longer exist if you work in the private sector, and the government now incentivizes you to save for your own retirement.

Depending on what type of organization you work for, there are
different names for this type of account. 401(k)s are for employees
of for-profit businesses, while 403(b)s do the exact same thing but
are for those working in nonprofits or tax-exempt organizations,
such as public schools.

Many employers will also "match" their employees' 401(k) contributions. To illustrate this, let's say you make $60,000 a year and
contribute to your company's 401(k). Your employer will match
up to 4% of your salary. This means that if you set aside $2,400 of
your salary into your 401(k) account annually, your employer will
give you an *additional* $2,400 in your account. It's a no-brainer
to contribute to get the full match of your employer because it's
literally *free* money!

Traditional vs. Roth 401(k)s

The best part about 401(k)s is that it's an entirely legal way to
lower your tax burden. There are two common options: traditional
401(k) and Roth 401(k).

- A **traditional 401(k)** allows you to contribute pre-tax
  money, meaning you can get an immediate tax break, and
  you'll get taxed on your earnings when you withdraw them
  in retirement after age 59½. This option is good if you're in
  a higher income tax bracket now and anticipate being in a
  lower tax bracket in retirement.

- A **Roth 401(k)** operates in reverse—you get taxed on your earnings from your job right away, you put away that money into the account, and once you retire, you can withdraw the money tax-free. If you're in a lower tax bracket now and believe you'll be in a higher tax bracket in the future, this could be a better option for you, because you'll pay taxes at a lower rate now and avoid potentially higher taxes on your withdrawals during retirement. However, choosing between traditional versus Roth 401(k) isn't necessarily a black-and-white decision. There may be factors unique to your situation, so do your research. Remember, personal finance is *personal*.

In 2025, the contribution maximum into a 401(k) is $23,500. This can change annually, primarily based on inflation, to help maintain purchasing power over time. 401(k) accounts typically offer a set number of funds you can invest in, so they're limited compared to other types of accounts in terms of what you're able to invest in.

IRAS

IRAs are another type of retirement account, but unlike 401(k)s, they are not tied to an employer. You can directly open up an IRA account on a brokerage site and start investing in any investment you wish that's available in the market. The requirement for contributing into an IRA is that you must be earning income in that given tax year.

Like 401(k)s, there are two types of IRAs: traditional and Roth. For traditional IRAs, the contributions are pre-tax, and you pay taxes on the amount that you withdraw in retirement. For Roth IRAs, you contribute post-tax earnings, and the growth is entirely tax-free.

But which one should you choose? Most financial experts recommend the Roth IRA over a traditional IRA because letting funds compound over a long period of time means that all the growth does not get taxed later on. Especially if you have a traditional 401(k) from your employer, diversifying various account types can provide you with more tax flexibility on how you want to withdraw your funds later on.

You can contribute up to $7,000 into your IRA in 2025, but make sure to check online, as this limit can change yearly. Also, Roth IRAs require you to be within a certain income limit in order to contribute to them. While traditional IRAs do not pose income limits, single filers making a full contribution to a Roth IRA in 2025 must have a modified adjusted gross income (MAGI) of less than $150,000. Joint filers are required to make less than $236,000 in order to make a full contribution. There is a phase-out where you can make partial contributions if you make equal or more than $150,000 but less than $165,000 as a single filer, or between $236,000 to $246,000 as joint filers. High-income earners who exceed these income limits can contribute to a Roth IRA through a loophole called the Backdoor Roth IRA.

TARGET DATE FUNDS

When your retirement savings are in a 401(k) or IRA, you may have the option to invest your money in a **target date fund**. These funds automatically adjust their investments over time based on how close you are to retirement. For example, let's say you were born in the year 2000 and choose a target date of 2065 fund. When you invest in a target date fund, the holdings will automatically shift as you age. From more aggressive, higher risk (but higher potential investments) when you're younger to more conservative, lower risk (but lower possible reward).

When you're younger, the fund is heavily concentrated in stocks, and it will start shifting toward a higher concentration of bonds as you approach retirement age. Target date funds are typically more conservative than stock funds, but they're good for people who prefer to have a fully automated retirement investing option.

Investing with an HSA

Even though medical costs might not be something you're actively thinking about, it's important to save for medical emergencies and for when you need the funds later down the line.

A way that you can do this is through a **Health Savings Account (HSA)**, a triple-tax advantaged savings account designed specifically for those who are under a high-deductible health plan (HDHP). You can use the money in this account for qualified medical expenses such as doctor's visits, medications, and even over-the-counter products like sunscreen. HSAs also act as a secondary retirement account where you can withdraw the money for non-medical expenses after age 65.

The magic behind HSAs is their triple-tax advantage: You don't pay taxes on the money you contribute, the earnings grow tax-free, and withdrawals for qualified medical expenses are tax-free. You can save a lot when using an HSA compared to paying for medical costs out-of-pocket. HSAs can also act as an investment account—you can invest your money to let it grow with the market.

For 2025, you can contribute up to $4,300 for self-only coverage and up to $8,550 for family coverage. Some employers also contribute to their employees' HSA accounts, so check to make sure what your employer's specific policies are.

There are also a few pitfalls to an HSA. Some states, like California and New Jersey, don't fully honor HSAs and tax their earnings (though they remain untaxed at the federal level). Also, an HDHP often comes with higher out-of-pocket costs before insurance kicks in, which may not work for everyone.

SELF-EMPLOYED RETIREMENT

Not everyone has a traditional job, and this is especially the case if you freelance or own your own business. If you fall into this category, you don't get 401(k) benefits from an employer, but there are still ways to save for retirement and reduce your tax liability.

If you are self-employed, you can open a **SEP-IRA (Simplified Employee Pension IRA)**, which is a retirement account for anyone who's self-employed, earns freelance income, or owns a business. You can contribute up to 25% of your net income (after deducting half of self-employment tax) or up to $70,000 in 2025, whichever is lower. The contributions are tax-deductible toward your business's revenue. But you will get taxed upon withdrawing the money in retirement (at age 59 1/2). I personally use a SEP-IRA to contribute to retirement through my business earnings.

Another option is a solo 401(k) or individual 401(k), which is designed for those who are self-employed (business owners with no employees). You're allowed to contribute up to $70,000 in 2025. In terms of tax advantages, you can pick between traditional or Roth, and the same tax rules apply here as discussed above in "401(k)s."

To open either type of account, you need to register for an **Employer Identification Number (EIN)** from the IRS website. This is used to identify your business in the tax system. It's a good way to separate your business finances from your personal finances. It's a very easy and quick process to receive this number once you register online.

ROLLING OVER YOUR RETIREMENT SAVINGS

If you are changing jobs (or anticipate doing so in the future), it's important to **rollover** your previous employer's 401(k) to your new employer's 401(k) or into a rollover IRA. This is so that you don't lose track of your funds and consolidate your savings.

A (not so) fun fact: Nearly 25% of all 401(k) assets are forgotten or left behind. You don't want this to be you.

Within 60 days of leaving your job, contact your old employer's plan administrator to request a direct rollover to your new 401(k) or rollover IRA so you avoid taxes or penalties. If you are rolling over funds into an IRA, you generally need to open a separate "rollover IRA" account, even if you already have an IRA account. This helps to separate 401(k) funds from your own contributions to an IRA.

WHAT HAPPENS IF YOU CASH OUT EARLY?

Ideally, the money that you put away for retirement shouldn't be touched until you actually retire. It's not a savings account where you can easily withdraw the money. Plus, most retirement accounts apply penalties for taking out funds early, but there are a few exceptions.

If you withdraw money from traditional accounts, it's taxed as ordinary income, and you pay a 10% penalty for early withdrawal (unless an exception applies). From Roth accounts, you can actually withdraw your initial contributions, aka. the money that you initially put in, tax-free at any time. But you can't withdraw the investment gains, or "profit," from the account. If you do, the earnings may be subject to income taxes and a 10% penalty unless the withdrawal is considered "qualified" (e.g., the account is held for at least five years and you're over 59½). However, you can withdraw from a Roth IRA penalty-free for first-time home purchases (up to $10,000), disability, and other specific circumstances like higher education expenses or medical emergencies. You can see an entire list of exceptions by looking up "PUB 590b IRS" online.

TAKEAWAYS
THE NEW RULES OF INVESTING

Investing's not just for the rich—with technology and free educational resources, it's never been more accessible to start growing your wealth in your twenties. You might not see progress tomorrow, but with time and consistency, you'll see promising growth that will set you up for years to come.

OLD RULES	NEW RULES
Investing is best left to finance experts	You can start investing yourself with a phone, funds, and solid research
You don't need to think about investing until you're set up in your thirties	It's never been more important to get a head start on investing to make the most of compound interest
Retirement funds are for older folks	Even small contributions to retirement in your twenties set you up for a more secure future
You should be debt-free before investing	With the right planning, it's possible to pay down debt while investing for the future
You can get rich fast with the right advice	Get-rich-quick financial gurus have multiplied in the internet age; if something seems too good to be true, it probably is

(8)

YOUR FINANCIAL FUTURE

So far, you've learned all the main elements of personal finance, from budgeting to managing your money and paying off debt. Within those ideas, you've been taught how to ditch your beliefs around money that hold you back so you can confidently invest in your future. You've come a long way from where you started, and it's now time to put your plan into action for the next phase of your financial journey.

Money management is a tool for building a life you love, whether you dream of being debt-free, owning a home, or traveling the world.

In this chapter, you will take a big step toward your financial future by implementing your learning. The goal is for you to make real progress toward your financial goals and create a future that aligns with your dream life.

YOUR FINANCIAL PRIORITIES

By now, you know all the components of personal finance. In the next section, we will examine your priorities. Depending on your situation, this will look different for everyone, but I've put together this list of priorities to help guide your decision-making:

1. Create a budget

2. Pay for essentials (rent, bills, food)

3. Build an emergency fund in high-yield savings account

4. Pay down high-interest debt (credit card debt)

**5. Contribute to a 401(k)
(up to employer match, if available)**

6. Save for short-term goals in high-yield savings account

7. Contribute to a Roth IRA

8. Invest (index funds, stocks, bonds)

**9. Make low-interest loan repayments
(student loan, home loan)**

UNDERSTANDING INSURANCE

You've likely heard of different kinds of **insurance**, but maybe you aren't quite sure how they work or if it's right for you at this stage in your life. Insurance helps protect you on various fronts when things don't go as planned: an illness, an accident, a natural disaster, theft, or otherwise. You pay a monthly or yearly fee, called a **premium**, to your insurer in exchange for a coverage plan. Then, if something goes wrong, the insurer will cover some or all of your expenses, depending on your plan. Some plans have a **deductible**, which you must pay before the insurer covers a claim. Here are the most common types of insurance.

Health insurance: In the U.S., you can stay on your parents' health insurance until you turn 26. U.S. health insurance is typically tied to an employer; you can enroll in when you get a job that offers a coverage plan. Another option to take advantage of the health insurance marketplace plan is to visit HealthCare.gov. The Affordable Care Act created this healthcare marketplace for people who did not have insurance through a job or had conditions that made it difficult for them to get insurance. Healthcare can get very costly, so you must be protected by a health insurance plan to ensure you get quality care.

Auto insurance: This is legally required to register and drive a car. It's also vital for accident protection and related costs. Your premium is based on various factors, including your age, the type of car you drive, and your driving record. Thankfully, premiums tend to go down as you reach your mid-twenties.

Renter's insurance: If you're renting an apartment, landlords are not legally required to cover theft or damage to your belongings. Renter's insurance does.

5 Signs You Are Doing Well Financially

The climb toward financial security can sometimes feel like a steep mountain, but don't forget to reflect on how far you've come! Even if you don't feel "rich" yet, here are five signs that you are doing better than you may realize:

1. **You're living within your means:** Financial health starts with spending less than you earn. This habit ensures you have the means to take care of your future self (pay yourself first), prevent yourself from going into debt, and invest in your goals.

2. **You have a plan to tackle your debt:** Creating and acting on your plan to pay down your debt means you're intentional about your future, making more room for saving and investing.

3. **You're investing for the future:** Even though saving is good, investing is how you build long-term wealth. Start investing early, no matter how small. As discussed in Chapter 7, the stock market is the easiest way to do this.

4. **You understand where your money goes:** Tracking your income and expenses helps you see your entire financial picture more clearly and is more effective at educating you about your spending habits. *You* are in control of your money.

5. **You've built a healthy credit score:** A good credit score helps you access more financial opportunities, like lower interest rates on mortgages and car loans.

YOUR FINANCIAL LIFE AFTER 30

Much of your financial life in your twenties revolves mainly around getting your footing around money and building a solid foundation. This can include starting your career, learning healthy money habits, paying off debt, and more. In your thirties, financial priorities tend to shift as you will likely want to expand the foundation you created in your twenties. It's also when many get married, start a family, and purchase a home. You likely will experience more upward growth in your career.

Ultimately, the principles of managing your finances don't change at this point in your life. Continue to review your monthly numbers (spending, debt, net worth), save and invest for the future, and work toward your financial goals. However, in your thirties, you'll ideally want to shift from a "saving" mindset to an "investing" mindset. The priority up to this point is creating a healthy financial foundation that covers your emergency fund and enough cash to cover your short- to medium-term goals. Ideally, high-interest debts, like credit card debt, are easily managed. You're able to pay off long-term loans, like student loans. By consistently putting extra funds into your investments, you're prioritizing and building long-term wealth that will serve you for years.

You'll likely also have more discretionary income as you progress in your career. It's tempting to upgrade your lifestyle as you make more; honestly, I'm all for it (within reason). I mean, not all of us want to live with roommates and have milk crates as furniture forever. Investing in parts of your lifestyle that are important to you will increase your quality of life and overall happiness, which is worth it. But be mindful of prioritizing your long-term goals and divvying up your resources wisely.

WHEN TO THINK ABOUT A FINANCIAL ADVISOR

You might also wonder whether you should seek outside help with your finances. While this is a highly personal decision, it's not uncommon for people with complex income or investment situations to seek help.

Hiring a **CPA (Certified Public Accountant)** can be great if you want to optimize your taxes during tax season. A CPA knows the tax rules and laws better than the average person and has valuable insights to help reduce your tax bill. Consider meeting with a **financial planner** to help you with specific questions and goals you may have. They will assess all your finances and help create a plan for long-term growth. Look for financial planners licensed as a Certified Financial Planner (CFP) and a fiduciary. This means they must act in the client's best interest and not what will make them the most commissions or fees. Not all financial planners are fiduciaries. Some may offer you suitable products, but they might not be the most cost-effective or in your best interest. Ask potential financial advisors if they're a fiduciary, their fee structure, and how they're compensated. For example, fee-only planners charge a flat fee or a percentage of their assets, while others may earn commissions from selling specific financial products.

YOUR WELL-BEING AND SELF-CARE

We've mainly discussed financial well-being, but emotional and physical well-being are worth exploring, if not more important. When pursuing your work and financial goals, it can be easy to neglect your mental health and overall well-being. A healthy balance between work and self-care is crucial to avoiding burnout.

It's easier than ever to have access to "work." The rise of remote work and tech devices allows you to work anywhere with an internet connection. The lines between work and life are increasingly blurred. I've been guilty of this myself. I spent many hours working late at night from my bed and not having time for much else.

Setting boundaries helps you draw a clear line between when it's time to work and when you're off the clock, so you can spend time with friends and family or have a little "me" time. I find that having dedicated personal time away from work is good for my mental health. It lets me mentally put away everything I did during the day and not think about it in the evening. One easy way to accomplish this is to find a designated area in your home for work. A desk in your living room, bedroom, or wherever will go a long way. I don't recommend working from your bed like I used to. Don't forget to schedule regular breaks between work sessions, and listen to your body. Rest *is* productive—you can't pour from an empty cup.

PLANNING FOR RETIREMENT

The average age that people retire in the U.S. is 62. So, it's understandable that the concept is not front and center of your mind right now. Hopefully, you're already taking steps to invest in retirement accounts, as we explored in the previous chapter.

The U.S. offers **Social Security** to citizens in retirement. It's a monthly check that helps cover living expenses. As of 2025, the average monthly benefit is $1,976. But that amount varies depending on the recipient, such as your earnings history, the age you started receiving retirement benefits, the number of years you worked, and other factors. This isn't a huge amount when considering what costs you may have later in life. All the more reason to start investing in your retirement young, even if it's just a little, to begin with—remember the magic of compound interest!

THE FIRE MOVEMENT

If you've spent any time in personal finance spaces online, you've probably seen people talking about a concept called

FIRE, or **Financial Independence Retire Early**. It involves a combination of intense budgeting and investing so you save enough money to retire early. The idea is that retirement is not an age but a *number* (how much you've saved and invested). If done right, FIRE creates financial independence that allows you to walk away from work (for the sake of income), pursue your passions, and have the freedom to design the life you want.

The FIRE movement focuses on aggressively saving and investing for long-term growth. To figure out how to achieve FIRE, multiply your annual living expenses by 25. This is also known as the 4% rule. For example, if your annual living expenses are $40,000, then you need $1 million invested to withdraw the money and still maintain the size of your portfolio.

The FIRE movement has its caveats. You will likely have to make extreme lifestyle sacrifices to save money, which can feel unsustainable over time. It's not for everyone.

Even if early retirement isn't your goal, FIRE principles are good for financial security: living within your means, maximizing savings, and prioritizing investing. Consider balancing these principles with traditional retirement strategies to create financial goals and a lifestyle that works well for you.

If you like the idea of pursuing your passions but FIRE isn't the right fit for you, another option is to take a sabbatical. Think of this as a career break where you take time to rest, take up personal projects, and travel. Paid sabbatical programs and those with progressive leave policies are more common in specific industries, like technology and healthcare. However, if your job doesn't offer a formal sabbatical program, you can still plan for one by saving up in advance or using unpaid leave. Remember that you'll need to budget for living expenses during this time, as most sabbaticals don't include a paycheck. No matter your approach, the fact that you're considering your retirement possibilities at a young age means you're ahead of the curve.

Helen Looks Ahead to Financial Success

Helen is a marketing manager who recently turned 30 and has diligently worked toward financial stability since she taught herself how to manage her money in her early twenties. As soon as she got her first job after graduating from college at age 22, Helen started contributing to her company's 401(k) plan. She also maxed out her Roth IRA annually, lived below her means, and prioritized gaining more experience to increase her earning potential. She started a successful side business as a brand and marketing consultant for companies she's passionate about. She balances saving for the future while enjoying the present and makes time and space in her budget for traveling and her hobbies.

At 30, Helen paid off her student loans, saved more than enough to cover costs for her first home, and created a six-figure investment portfolio by consistently contributing to low-cost index funds. She's accomplished a lot, but she's continuously motivated by the even bigger goals she's set for herself. She and her partner hope to achieve FIRE in their mid-forties to be work-optional. Even though she loves what she does, Helen doesn't want money to be something that holds her back from other things, such as taking extended time to travel or being able to leave a toxic workplace.

PUT IT INTO ACTION:
REVIEW YOUR FINANCIAL ROAD MAP

Remember when you created your financial road map in Chapter 1? It feels like an eternity ago, doesn't it? Since then, you've added new tools to your financial toolbox, and now's a good opportunity to revisit the first road map you made. Perhaps your perspective changed. Maybe you've switched around your goals after reading the other chapters in this book. It's a good idea to check in on your road map every couple of months, see your progress, and steer it in the right direction in the season of life you're in.

Take a look at the first road map you created earlier. Would you change anything about your goals now that you've read through the book? What new information did you learn that would be helpful for your financial journey moving forward? Write down any changes on the lines provided:

_____

_____

_____

_____

_____

_____

_____

Next, write down concrete steps you can take within three months to reach your goals. This will allow your subconscious mind to think and work toward *creating action*.

_____

_____

_____

_____

_____

_____

_____

_____

_____

_____

_____

Set up a calendar notification to check in on your road map every couple of months. As your life changes, your road map will change with you to reflect any new goals or changes in your life.

A FINAL NOTE

No matter your current financial situation, I sincerely hope this book has equipped you with the tools and knowledge you need to build the future you dream of and deserve. Gone are the days of financial information and tools being gatekept by the lucky few. I hope this book has empowered you with financial literacy and helped you consider fresh approaches to personal finance to set you up for a safer, more secure future.

Seeing positive changes in your finances might feel slow at first, whether you're just starting to pay off your debt or investing your money for the first time. Don't forget about compound interest. I keep bringing this up, but it's vital to growing your wealth. Putting away a little bit of money regularly will slowly evolve into something great. So be patient and enjoy the journey as much as you enjoy the destination. And don't forget that money is simply a tool to live your dream life, so keep a healthy balance!

Your financial journey is yours to shape. Stay curious, keep learning, and trust in your ability to achieve the life you dream of!

FINANCIAL RESOURCES

Books

I Will Teach You to Be Rich, by Ramit Sethi

The Psychology of Money, by Morgan Housel

The Simple Path to Wealth, by JL Collins

Websites

BLS.gov: The U.S. Bureau of Labor Statistics website provides wage estimates for various job titles.

Investopedia.com: A resource for investing education, personal finance, market analysis, and free trading simulators.

Investor.gov: Investing education and calculators provided by the U.S. Securities and Exchange Commission (official U.S. website).

IRS.gov: The official website of the Internal Revenue Service.

NerdWallet.com: A website with tools and advice for banking, credit cards, insurance, and mortgages.

Studentaid.gov: The Federal Student Aid website provides information about student grants and loans.

WSJ.com: *The Wall Street Journal* website covers the latest business and finance news.

REFERENCES

Chapter 1

Consumer Affairs. April 22, 2024. "Average American debt statistics 2025." consumeraffairs.com/finance/average-american-debt-statisitics.html.

Hanson, Melanie. January 15, 2025. "Student Loan Debt Statistics." Educational Data Initiative. educationdata.org/student-loan-debt-statistics#:~:text=The%20average%20federal%20student%20loan,financial%20quarter%20(2021%20Q4).

Seramount. February 13, 2024. "New Data Debunks Myths About Gen Z Workers." seramount.com/about-us/seramount-news-and-press/new-data-debunks-myths-about-gen-z-workers.

Chapter 2

Killingsworth, Matthew A.; Kahnemanb, Daniel; Mellers, Barbara. March 7, 2023. Proceedings of the National Academy of Sciences of the United States of America. "Income and emotional well-being: A conflict resolved." doi: 10.1073/pnas.2208661120.

Picchi, Aimee. March 10, 2023. "One study said happiness peaked at $75,000 in income. Now, economists say it's higher — by a lot." CBS News. cbsnews.com/news/money-happiness-study-daniel-kahneman-500000-versus-75000.

Chapter 3

The Association of Public and Land-grant Universities. Accessed January 29, 2025. "How does a college degree improve graduates' employment and earnings potential?" aplu.org/our-work/4-policy-and-advocacy/publicuvalues/employment-earnings. aplu.org/our-work/4-policy-and-advocacy/publicuvalues/employment-earnings.

Carnegie, Megan. BBC. June 28, 2023. "Why Gen Z are so motivated by pay" https://www.bbc.com/worklife/article/20230530-why-gen-z-are-so-motivated-by-pay.

Gillespie, Lane. Bankrate. July 10, 2024. "More than 1 in 3 Americans earn money through side hustles, 32% think they'll always need them." bankrate.com/credit-cards/news/side-hustles-survey.

Chapter 4

Caporal, Jack. October 18, 2024. Motley Fool Money. "2024 Buy Now, Pay Later Trends Study." fool.com/money/research/buy-now-pay-later-statistics.

Konish, Lorie. January 24, 2024. CNBC. "44% of Americans can't pay an unexpected $1,000 expense from savings." cnbc.com/2024/01/24/many-americans-cannot-pay-for-an-unexpected-1000-expense-heres-why.

Olya, Gabrielle. Yahoo Finance. February 23, 2024. "Why Are People Making 6 Figures Living Paycheck to Paycheck?" finance.yahoo.com/news/why-people-making-6-figures-150002458.html.

Chapter 5

Depietro, Andrew and Lapera, Gaby. April 29, 2024. Credit Kamara. "Average American debt by age and generation in 2023." https://www.creditkarma.com/insights/i/average-debt-by-age.

DeVon, Cheyenne. CNBC. March 27, 2024. "Here's how much credit card debt Americans have by age—and which generation owes the most." cnbc.com/2024/03/27/how-much-credit-card-debt-americans-have-by-age-html.

Federal Trade Commission. "Payday Lending." Accessed January 29, 2024. ftc.gov/news-events/topics/consumer-finance/payday-lending#:~:text=Many%20consumers%20who%20need%20cash,distressed%20consumers%20seeking%20these%20loans.

Parker, Kim and Igielnik, Ruth. Pew Research Center. May 14, 2020. "On the Cusp of Adulthood and Facing an Uncertain Future: What We Know About Gen Z So Far." pewresearch.org/social-trends/2020/05/14/on-the-cusp-of-adulthood-and-facing-an-uncertain-future-what-we-know-about-gen-z-so-far.

Sommer, Constance and Thangavelu, Poonkulali. Bankrate. February 14, 2024. "Average credit card debt in the U.S." bankrate.com/credit-cards/news/states-with-most-credit-card-debt.

Chapter 6

Cachero, Paulina and Ballentine, Claire. Bloomberg. September 20, 2023. "Nearly Half of All Young Adults Live With Mom and Dad — and They Like It." https://www.bloomberg.com/news/articles/2023-09-20/nearly-half-of-young-adults-are-living-back-home-with-parents?embedded-checkout=true.

Federal Student Aid. Accessed January 29, 2024. "5 Ways to Pay Off Your Student Loans Faster." studentaid.gov/articles/pay-off-student-loans-faster. studentaid.gov/articles/pay-off-student-loans-faster.

Guzman, Gloria and Kollar, Melissa. United States Census Bureau. September 10, 2024. "Income in the United States: 2023." https://www.census.gov/library/publications/2024/demo/p60-282.html.

Ludden, Jennifer and Wood, Daniel. NPR. June 20, 2024. "U.S. home prices have far outpaced paychecks. See what it looks like where you live." npr.org/2024/06/20/nx-s1-5005972/home-prices-wages-paychecks-rent-housing-harvard-report#:~:text=In%20past%20decades%2C%20it%20was,Philly%20is%20giving%20renters%20cash.

Chapter 7

Benson, Alana. Nerd Wallet. May 7, 2024. "What Is the Average Retirement Savings by Age?" nerdwallet.com/article/investing/the-average-retirement-savings-by-age-and-why-you-need-more.

Bieber, Christy. Yahoo Finance. December 4, 2024. "Americans forgot about $1.65 trillion in retirement savings — here's how to find and reclaim your lost money." finance.yahoo.com/news/americans-forgot-1-65-trillion-143300193.html.

Fidelity. Accessed January 29, 2025. "Should you pay down debt or invest?" fidelity.com/learning-center/personal-finance/pay-down-debt-vs-invest.

Hartman, Rachel; Brandon, Emily; and Walrack, Jessica. U.S. News & World Report. March 18, 2024. "What Is the Average Retirement Age in the U.S.?" money.usnews.com/money/retirement/aging/articles/what-is-the-average-retirement-age?

Iacurci, Greg. CNBC. June 7, 2023. "Crypto is Gen Z's most common investment. That may be risky, experts said." cnbc.com/2023/06/07/crypto-is-gen-zs-most-common-investment-that-may-be-risky.html.

Maverick, J.B. December 26, 2024. Ivestopedia. "S&P 500 average returns and historical performance." investopedia.com/ask/answers/042415/what-average-annual-return-sp-500.asp#:~:text=Inflation%20is%20one%20of%20the,understates%20the%20true%20inflation%20rate.

Royal, James and Barba, Mercedes. Bankrate. February 21, 2024. "When do most Americans take Social Security?" bankrate.com/retirement/when-do-most-americans-take-social-security.

Sommer, Jeff. April 14, 2023. The New York Times. "With the odds on their side, they still couldn't beat the market." nytimes.com/2023/04/14/business/stock-market-2022.html.

Chapter 8

Social Security. January 2, 2025. "What is the average monthly benefit for a retired worker?" ssa.gov/faqs/en/questions/KA-01903.html.

INDEX

business deductions, 59
retirement savings, 171
self-worth, 38
separate accounts, 66
SEP-IRAs, 171
shares, 145, 148
side hustles, 8, 50–51
smartphones, 3
snowball debt repayment
method, 98–99
socially responsible investing (SRI)
funds, 161
social media, 3, 6, 25, 83–84
Social Security, 180
spending
categorizing, 74–75
mindless vs. intentional, 25
prioritizing, 76
tracking, 73–74
ways to save, 82–83
state income taxes, 55
stock exchanges, 146
stock market, 145–146, 148
stock prices, 145
store credit cards, 107
student loans
about, 120
debt from, 2
delinquency and defaulting on, 125
federal, 120–122
fixed interest rates, 121
as good debt, 93
grace periods, 122
income-driven repayment plans, 122,
124–125
private, 122–123
refinancing, 124
repayment options, 121–122, 124–125
repayment planning, 127–128
tips for repaying, 123–124
subprime loans, 131
success, 38

T

target date funds, 169
taxes
breaks, 58–59
credits, 59, 142
filing, 59
filing status, 57
property, 140
rates, 56–57
student loan interest deductions, 124
types of, 55
W-4 form, 58
technology, 3, 8
trade schools, 45
traditional 401(k)s, 167
traditional IRAs, 168–169

U

upskilling, 11
USDA loans, 142
U.S. Department of Education, 120
U.S. Department of Labor, 54

V

VA loans, 141
Vanguard, 150–151
variable expenses, 75

W

W-4 form, 58
wage gaps, 3, 6
well-being, 179–180

Z

zero-based budgeting, 76

ABOUT THE AUTHOR

Lillian Zhang helps Gen Z and millennials navigate their finances through practical, relatable education that reaches and inspires hundreds of thousands across social media. A Silicon Valley professional and a graduate of the Haas School of Business at the University of California, Berkeley, she combines real-world experience with actionable financial guidance. She's been featured on *CNBC Make It*, *Business Insider*, *Bloomberg*, *ABC Good Morning America*, and *Yahoo Finance*. When not at her day job or creating content for her thriving TikTok, Instagram, and YouTube communities, Lillian enjoys exploring new cities, doing YouTube Pilates workouts, and hunting down the best local eats in the Bay Area.